LANGUAGE to GO

James Barry

Contributing Writer: Chelsea Donaldson

Review Panel

Lynn Archer
School District No. 36
Surrey, British Columbia

Carol Chandler
Halifax District School Board
Halifax, Nova Scotia

Rod Croskery
Carleton Place High School
Carleton Place, Ontario

Graham Foster
Calgary Roman Catholic Separate School
District, Calgary, Alberta

Gordon A. Francis
Ascension Collegiate
Bay Roberts, Newfoundland

Hamish Guthrie
White Oaks Secondary School
Oakville, Ontario

Ruth Knox
Wellington County Board of Education
Guelph, Ontario

Karen Newman
John Pritchard School
Winnipeg, Manitoba

Stefan Sierakowski
Lester B. Pearson Collegiate
Scarborough, Ontario

Dirk Verhulst
Kenner Collegiate Vocational Institute
Peterborough, Ontario

Nelson Canada

I(T)P An International Thomson Publishing Company

Toronto • Albany • Bonn • Boston • Cincinnati • Detroit • London • Madrid • Melbourne • Mexico City
New York • Pacific Grove • Paris • San Francisco • Singapore • Tokyo • Washington

I(T)P ™
International Thomson Publishing
The trademark ITP is used under license.

© Nelson Canada
A Division of Thomson Canada Limited, 1995

Published in 1995 by
Nelson Canada,
A Division of Thomson Canada Limited
1120 Birchmount Road
Scarborough, Ontario M1K 5G4

Adapted from material developed by
McDougal, Littell & Company

ISBN 0-17-604711-5

Canadian Cataloguing in Publication Data

Barry, James, 1939–
  Language to go

Includes index.
ISBN 0-17-604711-5

1. English language – Grammar. 2. English
language – Composition and exercises.
I. Donaldson, Chelsea, date. II. Title.

PE1112.B37 1994   425   C94-931669-5

Project Development: Joe Banel
Developmental Editor: Chelsea Donaldson
Associate Editor: Carolyn Madonia
Supervising Production Editor: Sandra Manley
Cover & Interior Design: Stuart Knox
Composition: Eva Zsigo, Frank Zsigo
Cover Illustration: Victor Gad
Interior Illustrations: Victor Gad

Printed and bound in Canada by Bryant Press.

·7890/BP/3

Acknowledgments

Every reasonable effort to trace the copyright
holders of materials appearing in this book has
been made. Information that will enable the publisher to rectify any error or omission will be wel-
comed. Acknowledgments accompanying certain
works constitute an extension of this copyright
page.

p. 21: "Harlem" from *The Panther and the Lash* by
Langston Hughes. Copyright 1951 by Langston
Hughes. Reprinted by permission of Alfred A.
Knopf, Inc. / p. 50: "First Political Speech" by Eli
Mandel reprinted courtesy of the estate of Eli
Mandel. / p. 51: excerpt from *Paddle to the Amazon*
by Don Starkell and Charles Wilkins used by permission of the Canadian Publishers, McClelland
& Stewart, Toronto. / p. 70: Nestlings cartoon
reproduced with permission of the cartoonist. /
p. 105: poem by Jan Krasnodebski used by permission. / p. 115: Nestlings cartoon reproduced
with permission of the cartoonist. / p. 120 excerpt
from *Mark My Words: The Memoirs of a Very
Political Reporter* © 1992 by Marjorie Nichols,
published by Douglas & McIntyre. Reprinted by
permission. / pp. 128 and 130: excerpts from
Water Monsters by Alan Garinger, a Volume in the
Great Mysteries series, © 1992 by Greenhaven
Press, Inc., San Diego, California. Used by
permission.

This book is printed on acid-free paper, approved
under Environment Canada's "Environmental
Choice Program." The choice of paper reflects
Nelson Canada's goal of using, within the
publishing process, the available resources,
technology, and suppliers that are as environment
friendly as possible.

Using *Language to Go*

Language to Go is a book about communication—about writing clearly and correctly. We hope *Language to Go* will help you improve your writing and editing skills.

Use this book as a handy reference when you want to polish your work. *Language to Go* can help you correct common errors in grammar, word usage, sentence structure, punctuation, and other language conventions. For example:

- You can use the **Checklist** of common problems in language that appears on the inside back cover for quick reference to help you identify areas for improvement.
- If you know you have difficulty with a particular topic— for example, run-on sentences— look it up in the **Index** at the back. The Index will refer you to the appropriate page, in this case to an explanation of sentences as complete thoughts.
- **Exercises** throughout, with answers at the back, give you the chance to work independently to confirm your understanding.

We hope this book will help make your writing "go," and that you will have some fun along the way.

The Parts of Speech

All words in our language are classified into eight groups called the parts of speech.

Although there are over half a million words in the English language, every word belongs to one or more of the eight parts of speech when that word is used in a sentence.

The Eight Parts of Speech

The BIG FOUR	The Little Four
1. Noun	5. Pronoun
2. Verb	6. Preposition
3. Adverb	7. Conjunction
4. Adjective	8. Interjection

The Big Four

1. **Noun** A noun is a word that names a person, place, thing, or idea.

    Examples scientist Mars telescope equality time
    The *scientists* studied *Mars* through the *telescope*.

2. **Verb** A verb is a word that expresses an action or a state of being. Verb forms usually change to show the time of the action.

    Examples cook swoop dive is exist does
    A pelican *swooped* down and *dived* into the water.

3. **Adverb** An adverb is a word that modifies a verb, an adjective, or another adverb. It tells where, when, how, or to what extent.

   Examples suddenly often beautifully also
   Often the bird would *suddenly* start singing *beautifully*.

4. **Adjective** An adjective is a word that modifies, or defines by describing, a noun or a pronoun. It tells which one, how many, what kind, or how much. Often, it comes before the noun it modifies.

   Examples green smart some extraordinary
   Megumi's *green talking* parrot has *extraordinary* feathers.

The Little Four

5. **Pronoun** A pronoun is a word used in place of a noun or another pronoun.

   Examples she we yourself nobody who everybody
   "Just be *yourself*," *she* said. "*We* want *you* to feel at home."

6. **Preposition** A preposition is a word that shows how a noun or pronoun is related to some other word in the sentence. Many prepositions indicate direction, position, or relation in time.

   Examples across at of until in about from on
   Across the creek *at* the edge *of* the field stood a deer.

7. **Conjunction** A conjunction is a word that connects words or groups of words.

   Examples and or but so yet because if
   Peoples of ancient Egypt, Central America, *and* South America all built pyramids, *but* they developed the pyramid idea independently.

8. **Interjection** An interjection is a word or group of words that show feeling or sudden emotion. An interjection can stand by itself.

   Examples wow hey my word oh, well
   Hey! That was a shooting star!

Another Way of Looking at It

Another way of grouping the parts of speech is as follows:

Group 1 Words that name (persons, places, things, ideas, qualities):
- *nouns*
- *pronouns*

Group 2 Words that modify:
- *adjectives*
- *adverbs*

Group 3 Action words:
- *verbs*

Group 4 Linking and connecting words:
- *conjunctions*
- *prepositions*

Group 5 Added words that express feeling:
- *interjections*

Parts of Speech at a Glance

Each word in a sentence is a specific part of speech. The numbers underneath the words in the following sentences indicate which of the eight parts of speech each is.

Oh, Carmine and I often told funny stories at summer
8   1   7 5 3 2   4   1 6   4
camp.
  1

Whew! Although I am nothing but a conjunction out
 8   7   5 2   1   7 4   1   6
of control, I still have my sentence written correctly.
6   1   5 3   2 4   1   2   3

Colourless green ideas sleep furiously.
  4   4   1   2   3

Source Note

This nonsense sentence was coined by famous language expert Noam Chomsky.

Exercise 1   *Identifying Parts of Speech*

Each of the following sentences is the first line of a story or book. Which of them make you interested to read more? Identify the part of speech of each of the underlined words.

1. As <u>Gregor</u> Samsa awoke one morning from <u>uneasy</u> dreams <u>he</u> found himself transformed in his bed <u>into</u> a gigantic insect. ("The Metamorphosis," Franz Kafka)

2. It <u>was</u> a bright cold day <u>in</u> April, and the clocks were striking thirteen. (*1984*, George Orwell)

3. <u>O</u> for a Muse of fire, that would ascend
The brightest heaven of invention;
A kingdom for a stage, princes to act
And <u>monarchs</u> to behold the swelling scene!
(*Henry V*, William Shakespeare)

4. Dad came down with the flu that week, <u>so</u> I had to go <u>down</u> to the subway and feed the <u>unicorns</u>. ("Midnight Snack," Diane Duane)

5. "No question of it," Mr. Archipelago said, <u>delicately</u> snipping a wisp of hair. "<u>I</u> am flotsam." ("The Perfume Sea," Margaret Laurence)

6. It was a dark <u>and</u> stormy night ... (*Paul Clifford*, Edward Bulwer-Lytton)

7. Long ago there was a giant <u>who</u> loved to kill humans, <u>eat</u> their flesh, and drink their blood. ("How Mosquitoes Came to Be," retold by Richard Erdoes and Alfonso Ortiz)

8. When I hear the rain lashing against my window, their <u>cries</u> come back to me <u>once</u> again, those cries that used to stick to my skin like leeches. ("Haute Cuisine," Ampero Dávila, trans. Alberto Manguel)

9. Lisa Barnett, moving down the halls, books clasped against her chest, tosses <u>tawny</u> hair <u>away</u> from her eyes in one fluid motion. ("The Crystal Stars Have Just Begun to Shine," Martha Brooks)

10. The sea burst <u>against</u> the bow where Bill lay on the starboard bunk, and the boat timbers shivered and trembled the full ten-metre length of the *Pacific Maid*. ("Troller," Kevin Roberts)

Writing Tip

The first line of a piece of writing is extremely important. It is what hooks your readers and makes them want to read more. Which one of these first lines grabs your attention most? Why? What would you expect the rest of the story to be like?

Exercise 2 *Drafting Skill*

Write five serious and five nonsense sentences with as many of the parts of speech as you can incorporate into each. Place the corresponding number of the correct part of speech underneath each word in your sentences.

Example   Oh, the wildebeests of Africa never let rainy days and
        8   4   1   6   1   3   2   4   1   7

        Mondays depress them.
           1   2   5

Writing Complete Sentences

A sentence is a group of words that expresses a complete thought. Every sentence contains a verb, begins with a capital letter, and ends with a period, a question mark, or an exclamation point.

Not just any group of words can stand as a sentence. Here are some types of word groups that are not sentences.

Phrases

A phrase is a group of related words that does not contain a verb. Phrases often begin with a preposition such as *in*, *of*, *through*, *at*, or *under*, and end with a noun.

> to the ends of the earth   under the sea

Clauses

Clauses are groups of related words that have a subject and a verb, and that form part of a sentence.

A **subordinate clause** cannot stand on its own as a sentence because it does not express a complete thought. It needs other words to complete its meaning and make a complete sentence.

Subordinate Clause	as we watched
Sentence	As we watched, the sun rose.
Subordinate Clause	because the weather was so bad
Sentence	School was cancelled because the weather was so bad.
Subordinate Clause	that ate the rat
Sentence	This is the cat that ate the rat.

Verbal Phrases

Another type of phrase is a verbal phrase. Verbals are words that are formed from verbs, but which function in a sentence as other parts of speech, such as nouns, adjectives, or adverbs.

Speaking well *is a lost art.*
Beaten and tired, *he gave up the fight.*
I forgot *to write it down.*

(There is more information about verbal phrases in Section 5, "Using Modifiers.")

A **principal clause** expresses a complete thought and contains a subject and a verb. The only thing you need to make a principal clause into a sentence is correct punctuation.

Principal Clause	to err is human
Sentence	To err is human.
Principal Clause	let go of my nose
Sentence	Let go of my nose!
Principal Clause	what is that
Sentence	What is that?

Exercise 1   *Recognizing Sentences*

Tell whether each of the following is a phrase or a clause. For those clauses that could stand alone as sentences, add the necessary punctuation.

1. around the back

2. that I loved once

3. Irina fixed

4. if he calls

5. it was the seafood

6. never in a million years

7. speaking softly

8. give me a call

9. legends that reflect the beliefs

10. rehearse your interviewing techniques

Sentence Parts at a Glance

The **complete subject** includes all the words that identify the person, place, thing, or idea the sentence is about.

The **complete predicate** includes all the words that tell or ask something about the subject.

The Canadian **skater won** her event.

The **simple subject** tells exactly whom or what the sentence is about. It may be one word or a group of words, but it does not include modifiers.

The **simple predicate,** or verb, tells what the subject does or is. It may be one word or several, but it does not include modifiers.

An **indirect object** is a word or a group of words that tells *to whom* or *for whom* or *to what* or *for what* about the verb. A sentence can have an indirect object only if it has a direct object. The indirect object always comes before the direct object in a sentence.

A **compound subject** has two or more parts connected with a **coordinating conjunction** such as *and*. Note that verbs, objects, and predicates can also be compound.

The **Canadians** and **Germans were giving** the **French** some **competition**.

Verbs often have more than one part. They may be made up of a **main verb**, like *giving*, and one or more **auxiliary**, or **helping, verbs** like *were*.

A **direct object** is a word or group of words that tells *who* or *what* receives the action of the verb in a sentence.

Subjects and Predicates

Every group of words that forms a sentence has a subject and a predicate. The subject is the person or thing that the sentence is about. The predicate tells something about the subject.

Subject	Predicate
Sarah McLachlan	sang.
We were	cheering.

Each of the sentences above contains only a **simple subject** and a **simple predicate**, or **verb**, with no modifiers. A sentence may also have other elements, such as objects, that complete its meaning. Being able to recognize the subject and predicate of a sentence makes it much easier to understand how all the parts of the sentence relate to each other.

Finding the Subject

The simple subject is the precise person(s), place(s), thing(s), or idea(s) that the sentence is about.

The simple subject (ss) always contains a noun or a pronoun, or a word acting as a noun. It never contains adjectives, adverbs, or other words that describe or limit. To find the simple subject, ask yourself exactly whom or what the sentence is about.

ss

Renata swam.

ss

My *bike* with the broken fenders was stolen!

ss

Carla and *Stephan* sold their house.

The complete subject includes all the words that identify the person(s), place(s), thing(s), or idea(s) that the sentence is about.

The simple subject (ss) is always part of the complete subject. Sometimes, the simple subject and the complete subject are the same.

Bicycles are very practical.

Compound Subjects

If a simple subject consists of more than one person or thing connected by a comma or a word like and, *it is called a **compound simple subject**, or simply a **compound subject**.*

Other times, the complete subject contains the simple subject along with adjectives, adverbs, or other words or phrases that modify (describe) the subject.

complete subject

The streets of the old town were deserted.

ss

complete subject

The man who won the pie-eating contest felt very ill.

ss

Finding the Predicate

The simple predicate is the verb or verbs that tell what the subject does or is.

To find the simple predicate (or verb) in a sentence, find the complete subject and ask *what?*

> Alphonso *mashed* his peas.
> (Alphonso what? He *mashed*.)

> Jaime *is* no taller than a giraffe on stilts.
> (Jaime what? He *is*.)

> Raisa *woke* up and *smelled* the coffee.
> (Raisa what? She *woke* and *smelled*.)

The simple predicate is always a verb, but don't assume that all the verbs in a sentence are part of the simple predicate. Only verbs that answer *what?* about the subject are part of the simple predicate.

> I *like* the skirt that Savitsa wore.
> (*Like* is the simple predicate, because it answers *what?* about the subject *I*.
> The verb *wore* describes what *Savitsa* did, not what *I* did.)

> The coat that Ganesh bought *is* not very warm.
> (*Is* is the simple predicate, because it answers *what?* about the subject *coat*.
> The verb *bought* answers *what?* about *Ganesh*, not the coat.)

Compound Predicates

When a simple predicate contains two or more verbs connected by a word like and, *it is called a* **compound simple predicate**, *or simply a* **compound predicate**.

Clauses

In the example, I like the skirt *is a principal clause, and* that Savitsa wore *is a subordinate clause. A verb in a subordinate clause is never the simple predicate of the sentence.*

14

How can you find the simple predicate in a sentence with more than one verb if you are not sure of the subject? Try breaking it up into smaller sentences, or clauses, with one verb in each. Then decide which sentence is closest in meaning to the original.

The compact disc I played was damaged.
(The compact disc was damaged. I played the compact disc.)

The compact disc was damaged is closer in meaning to the original, so *was*, not *played*, is the simple predicate, and *compact disc* is the simple subject.

Some words that look like verbs act as other parts of speech, such as nouns, adjectives, or adverbs. A verb that does not function as a verb cannot be the simple predicate.

Watching basketball is my favourite sport.
(The simple predicate is *is*; *watching* acts as a subject.)

She found broken glass in her cereal box.
(The simple predicate is *found*; *broken* acts as an adjective describing *glass*.)

He plays to win.
(The simple predicate is *plays*; *win* acts as an adverb describing *plays*.)

A verb with *to* added on the front cannot act as a simple predicate. A verb with *-ing* added on to it cannot act as a verb unless it has a helping verb such as *be* or *have* in front.

The complete predicate includes all the words that tell or ask something about what the subject does or is.

The complete predicate includes the simple predicate along with any other words or groups of words that modify or describe it.

complete predicate
⌐———¬
John spoke.

complete predicate
⌐—————————————————¬
The mountain rumbled and shook mightily.
           └——————————————┘
                   sp

A word or group of words that relates to the simple subject will answer a question put in front of the simple subject (*what* man? *which* house? *what kind of* animal? *how many* cars?). A word or group of words that belongs to the predicate answers a question put after the simple predicate (ran *where?* ate *what?* is *who?* lived *when?*).

complete subject   complete predicate

The mug that I liked best | was hanging on the shelf that collapsed.
    ss   sp

That I liked best is part of the subject because it relates to the simple subject *mug* (*which* mug?). *On the shelf that collapsed* is part of the predicate because it relates to the simple predicate *was hanging* (was hanging *where?*).

Exercise 2   *Finding Subjects and Predicates*

Rewrite the following sentences, underlining the complete subject once and the complete predicate twice. Then write the simple subject (ss) and simple predicate (sp).

1. Europe and the United States produce most board games played in Canada.

2. One notable exception is the board game called *Trivial Pursuit*.

3. This game, which has been extremely successful, was invented by a group of Canadians in the early 1980s.

4. Since then, it has been copied and sold all over the world.

5. All of the people who originally invested in the game are now millionaires.

6. Many versions of the original game are available, aimed at people of different ages and with different interests.

7. Each member of a team answers trivia questions and moves a game piece around a board.

8. Winning or losing is less important than having fun and learning a thing or two!

9. We like to take turns asking the questions while everyone else guesses the answers.

10. Thanks to the success of *Trivial Pursuit*, game inventing is flourishing in Canada.

Sentence Fragments

A sentence fragment is a group of words that does not express a complete thought.

A group of words is a fragment if it is punctuated like a sentence, but additional words are required in order to complete the idea. You can correct a sentence fragment by adding the missing words.

Fragment   Spent twenty years in a South African jail.
(*Who* or *what* spent twenty years in jail? The subject is missing.)

Sentence   Nelson Mandela spent twenty years in a South African jail.

Fragment   Wandering around downtown.
(*What* happened while wandering around downtown? *Who* was wandering? Additional words are needed to complete the idea.)

Sentence   Wandering around downtown, we came upon a great little restaurant.

Fragment   The Komodo dragons in Indonesia.
(*What about* the Komodo dragons? The verb is missing.)

Sentence   The Komodo dragons in Indonesia like to bask in the sun all day.

> ### Writing Tip
>
> *In some situations the rule against using fragments can be broken:*
>
> - *Fragments are acceptable in conversation and in written dialogue (which is, after all, an imitation of conversation).*
> - *We often answer questions with an incomplete sentence or a one-word reply.*
> - *When taking notes you probably use fragments because you don't have time to write complete sentences.*

Quick Tip

To check for sentence fragments in a composition, try reading the last sentence aloud, then the next to the last sentence, and so on. By reading the sentences in reverse order, you can concentrate on each by itself. When reading each sentence, ask yourself, does this group of words express a complete thought?

The Secrets of the Great Authors Revealed!

Looking back, I imagine I was always writing. Twaddle it was too. But better far write twaddle or anything, anything, than nothing at all.

Katherine Mansfield (short story writer)

Just get it down on paper, and then we'll see what to do with it.

Maxwell Perkins (publisher and editor)

There's nothing to writing. All you do is sit down at a typewriter and open a vein.

Red Smith (sports writer)

Learn to write in five easy lessons.

1. Start writing. Concern yourself with style, mechanics, persona later.

2. Rewrite.

3. Rewrite.

4. Rewrite.

5. Rewrite.

So when I say "work," I only mean writing. Everything else is just odd jobs.

Margaret Laurence (writer)

When I stepped from hard manual work to writing, I just stepped from one kind of hard work to another.

Sean O'Casey (dramatist)

Most of the basic material a writer works with is acquired before the age of fifteen.

Willa Cather (writer)

Exercise 3   *Sentence Fragments*

On your paper, write each group of words. If the word group is a sentence, add the necessary capitalization and end punctuation. If the word group is a fragment, add whatever is necessary to make it a complete sentence.

Example   a stand-up comedian
Answer   A stand-up comedian has a difficult job.

1. make people laugh

2. come up with original gags and funny stories

3. many never make the big time

4. in comedy clubs around the country

5. after a comedian has appeared on television

6. attend acting schools or simply learn by watching other comedians

7. tricks of the trade, such as raising one's voice at the end of a punch line

8. every comic must contend with hecklers

9. learn what to do and say when there are hecklers in the audience

10. the best way to deal with a heckler

Exercise 4　*More Sentence Fragments*

See if you can decode the following platespeak messages. Then identify which of the messages are complete sentences, and which are fragments.

Platespeak

Platespeak is the language used on personalized licence plates. It uses letters, numbers, and words to spell out messages. The term "platespeak" was coined by Daniel Nussbaum, a humour writer and location scout.

Answers

1. I see you 2. I be for you or I before you 3. are you moving 4. I hate smog
5. no brakes 6. anyone for tennis 7. tea for two 8. get with it 9. paradise
10. well kept

Run-on Sentences

Stay Tuned...

Often, run-on sentences are simple, choppy thoughts that can be combined and written as one sentence. For more on how to combine sentences, see Section Eight, "Sentence Combining."

A run-on sentence is two or more sentences written as one.

Run-ons occur when writers include too many thoughts in a sentence. You can avoid confusing run-on sentences by putting a period or other end mark at the end of each complete sentence. Of course, each sentence should begin with a capital letter.

Run-on   The catcher gave the signals then the pitcher started to sweat.

Correct   The catcher gave the signals. Then the pitcher started to sweat.

Run-ons also occur when writers use commas instead of periods, colons, or semicolons to separate complete thoughts. When a writer uses a comma between two sentences, he or she commits the error known as a comma splice or comma fault. Correct a comma splice in the same way you would correct any other run-on.

Comma Splice   A helicopter arrived, it rescued the flood victims.

Correct   A helicopter arrived. It rescued the flood victims.

Exercise 5   *Run-on Sentences*

Correct the following sentences that are run-ons by adding capitalization and punctuation to show where each complete thought begins and ends. If a sentence is not a run-on, write "correct."

Example   Long ago in South America, the Incas ruled a vast empire, it stretched for most of the length of South America.

Answer   Long ago in South America, the Incas ruled a vast empire. It stretched for most of the length of South America.

1.   The great period of the Inca empire began when a neighbouring nation threatened to invade Inca land, the Incas met their neighbours on the battlefield and overpowered them.

2. When they conquered an area, the Incas enlisted its men into their army, thus the Inca army grew to mighty proportions.

3. By the late 1400s the empire was at its height its ruler was named Huayna Capac.

4. Huayna Capac had two sons, the older, Huáscar, was supposed to become ruler of the Incas after his father died, but Huayna Capac gave half the empire to the younger son, Atahualpa.

5. After Huayna Capac died, the two brothers declared war on each other each raised an enormous army.

6. Their battles left thousands of warriors dead, finally Atahualpa defeated Huáscar for good in a great battle.

7. While Atahualpa was relaxing after the battle, he heard a strange report, some odd-looking bearded men had arrived.

8. The Incas had never seen Europeans before, they thought that Francisco Pizarro and his Spanish conquistadors must be gods.

9. Pizarro captured Atahualpa and held him for ransom, he promised to release the Inca king if his subjects would fill a ransom room with gold.

10. The Incas filled the room with gold, however, Pizarro simply took the gold and killed the Inca leader anyway.

Exercise 6   *Complete Sentences*

Tell whether each group of words is a complete sentence, sentence fragment, or run-on sentence. Then rewrite the paragraph without fragments or run-ons. Add or delete words, capitalization, and punctuation as necessary.

1. Langston Hughes, one of the leading writers of the Harlem Renaissance

2. Born in 1902 in Joplin, Missouri, at the beginning of a new century and of a new age in African-American culture

3. From an early age, he devoured the poetry of Carl Sandburg and Walt Whitman, he himself began publishing poetry at the age of nineteen

4. Hughes studied at Columbia University after one year he left school and became a sailor on a freighter

---

Harlem

What happens to a
dream deferred?
Does it dry up
like a raisin in the sun?
Or fester like a sore—
And then run?
Does it shrink like rotten
meat?
Or crust and sugar over
like a syrupy sweet?
Maybe it just sags
like a heavy load.
Or does it explode?

Langston Hughes

5. Hughes ended up in Paris there he listened to jazz in crowded nightclubs

6. Hughes's first book of poetry was published in 1926 that same year Hughes enrolled at Lincoln University

7. Hughes's first novel, *Not Without Laughter*, portrayed everyday African-American life it was a great success

8. In 1939, he founded the Harlem Suitcase Theater

Exercise 7   *Sentence Review*

Tell whether each group of words is a complete sentence, sentence fragment, or run-on sentence. Correct the fragments by adding words to make complete sentences. Correct the run-ons, including comma splices, by adding capitalization and punctuation.

1. The Cambrian period of geology began around 570 million years ago

2. Lasted for about 70 million years

3. For millions of years, only very simple life forms such as worms and anemones

4. Then a huge explosion of animal evolution took place, in the space of a mere 10 million years virtually all the different phyla, or body types, came into being

5. The Burgess Shale in the Canadian Rockies contains countless fossils dating from the Cambrian period, some animals found there have no living descendants

6. Others are primitive ancestors of animals still in existence, a lot of the animals look like something out of a horror movie

7. Among the strange fossil creatures the tulip-shaped Dinomischus and Hallucigenia, a wormlike animal with spikes along its back and short spiky legs

8. Perhaps the most significant discovery among the fossils of the Burgess Shale is Pikaia

9. Pikaia, a worm no bigger than your pinky finger, with the beginnings of a spinal column

10. This unassuming little fellow is our own ancestor, we certainly have come a long way

The Evolution of English: Words from Other Languages

Languages change and evolve just as animals and people do. English has evolved by borrowing words from languages around the world. See if you can name the language that gave us each of these sets of words:

1. blasé, gourmet, potpourri, queue

2. cruise, yacht, skate, deck

3. vodka, cosmonaut, intelligentsia, rouble

4. etymology, narcotic, euphemism, analysis

5. opera, solo, studio, tempo, violin

6. sofa, tiger, shawl, caravan, pyjamas

7. silk, cash, tea, ketchup, chop suey

8. algebra, zero, assassin, giraffe

9. amen, shalom, cherub, jubilee

10. kindergarten, hamburger, delicatessen, lager

Foreign Expressions

Here are some foreign expressions used in everyday English.

Adios (Spanish)
goodbye
à la carte (French)
items on menu are all priced separately
alter ego (Latin)
other personality
savoir faire (French)
knowing how to act
siesta (Spanish)
short nap

Answers
1. French 2. Dutch 3. Russian 4. Greek 5. Italian 6. Persian
7. Chinese 8. Arabic 9. Hebrew 10. German

Using Nouns

A noun is a word that names a person, place, thing, or idea.

Persons Rick Hansen, aunt, teacher
Places Vancouver, river, museum, Saturn
Things camera, coat, book, pencil
Ideas hope, justice, truth, prejudice

Creative Collective Nouns

a flight of swallows
a parliament of owls
a span of mules
a hatch of flies
a yammer of radio announcers
a grouse of ball players
a conceit of managers

Create your own!

a _____ of students
a _____ of school buses

Noun Classes

Nouns can be classified into six groups.

Common Noun A general name, such as *city, game, palace, lake, writer.*

Proper Noun A specific name, such as *Edmonton, Grey Cup, Buckingham Palace, Roberta Bondar, The Rolling Stones.* Note that proper nouns are always capitalized.

Concrete Noun Anything that can be seen, heard, smelled, touched, or tasted, such as *cashews, smoke, fern, bell.*

Abstract Noun Something that cannot be directly seen, heard, touched, tasted, or smelled, such as *courage, idea, peacefulness, duty.*

Compound Noun A noun made of two or more words, such as *earthworm, great-uncle, ice hockey, Main Street.* Some compounds are written as one word, some as two words, and others with a hyphen.

Collective Noun A noun that names a group of people or things, such as *Inuit, committee, family, society, class, team.*

Be Precise!

Use nouns that tell your reader something about your subject.

For example, you could say:

> He lived in a house with a dog and a cat.

But you give a better visual picture if you say:

> He lived in a mansion with a Doberman and a Persian blue.
>
> OR
>
> He lived in a bungalow with a beagle and a tabby.

Using a Thesaurus

A good way to find nouns that are more specific is to use a thesaurus. A **thesaurus** *is a book that lists synonyms (words that mean the same thing, or almost the same thing) and antonyms (words that mean the opposite of each other).*

Noun Usage at a Glance

An **indirect object** tells to whom or for whom something is done or given.

A **direct object** tells who or what receives the action of the verb.

Dr. Doolittle gave the **lion** some **medicine** in the **evening**.

A **subject** is the person, place, thing, or idea that the sentence is about.

An **object of a preposition** comes after a preposition such as *in, of, at, on, to,* or *for*.

Prepositions are small words that introduce phrases. Often one of the words that follow a preposition is a noun.

at the *movies*	for *Paula*	around *town*	to the *dregs*
down the *road*	over the *hill*	through the *bog*	under the *weather*

Plural Nouns

Most nouns form the plural by simply adding *-s* or *-es* to the singular.

> waltz/waltzes   dance/dances   step/steps

However, there are quite a few exceptions to this rule. Some nouns change their spelling slightly in the plural.

> loaf/loaves   party/parties   crisis/crises

Others do not change at all, or form the plural in a unique way.

> moose/moose   man/men
> mouse/mice   medium/media

If you are unsure about how to form the plural of a noun, look it up in the dictionary.

Plurals of Compound Nouns

If a compound noun is hyphenated or written as separate words, change the most important word to the plural form. If it is written as one word, change the last word to the plural form.

bill-of-sale/bills-of sale
rosebush/rosebushes
shovelful/shovelfuls

The Tale of a Prints

How many spelling errors can you find in this story?

The tail I tell is of a small prints, air to a thrown,
who won day went fission with sum of the guise.
On they're weigh to the stream they past a rabid whole.
Wanting to ketch the rabid four diner, they set out
sum lattice, sum salary, and sum garrets four hymn.
The hair was two smart four the men, and escaped buy
a latter he had mate at the back of his burrow.
The prints gave up, disappointed that he could knot
have meet four diner that knight. He hoped that the fish
wood find the bait he had brought more tempting.
But the choke was on the prints, four the fish just swam
away threw the weeds and ignored the danger above on
the service of the water.

Know More Miss Takes

I have a spelling checker.
It came with my PC.
It plainly marks four my
  revue
Miss Steaks I cannot sea.
I've run this poem threw it,
I'm sure your pleased to no.
It's letter perfect in its
  weigh;
My checker tolled me sew.

Answers

tale, prince, heir, throne | one, fishing, some, guys | their way, rabbit hole | catch, rabbit for dinner | some lettuce, some celery, some carrots for him | hare, too, for, by | ladder, made | prince, not | meat for dinner, night | would | joke, prince, for | through | surface

Possessive Nouns

A **possessive noun** is one that shows ownership or belonging. Follow these rules when forming the possessives of nouns:

1. **If a noun is singular, add an apostrophe and -*s* to form the possessive.**
    Solveg's book   winter's chill
    the cobra's smile   Ms. Ruiz's husband

2. **If a noun is plural and ends in -*s*, add just the apostrophe.**
    parents/parents' advice   players/players' coaches

3. **If a noun is plural and does not end in -*s*, add an apostrophe and -*s*.**
    geese/geese's feathers   women/women's sports

> ### The Choice Is Yours
>
> *Sometimes, instead of writing a possessive using an apostrophe, you may want to use a prepositional phrase. A prepositional phrase consists of a preposition, such as at or of, and an object. For example, instead of writing* the mongoose's fur, *write* the fur of the mongoose.

Writers often confuse the rules for plurals and possessives. Remember that adding an apostrophe to a noun will never make it plural.

Exercise 1   *Possessive Nouns*

Write the possessive form of the underlined word in the singular or plural as indicated. Then write a sentence using the possessive form or an equivalent prepositional phrase (whichever sounds better).

Item   the <u>speaker</u> (singular) message
Answer   the speaker's message

          The speaker's message was, "The planet needs your help."

          OR

          The message of the speaker was, "The planet needs your help."

1. the <u>pitcher</u> (plural) gloves

2. <u>Navroz</u> (singular) answer

3. the <u>radio</u> (plural) prices

4. an <u>actress</u> (singular) career

5. two <u>grandchild</u> (plural) pictures

Mnemonic Spelling

And Remember...

If it sounds like me, *it's* i *before* e, *except after* c. *There are some exceptions to this rule:* weird, seize, leisure, neither, either. *Now, think of a mnemonic sentence to remind you of the odd ones out. For example,* Neither is it weird to seize leisure, either!

Mnemonics (pronounced nu-MON-iks) are memory devices you can use to remind you how to spell words such as February and whether to write stationary or stationery. Mnemosyne was the goddess of memory in Greek mythology.

balloon	Remember the **ball** in b**all**oon.
believe	You can't bel**ie**ve a **lie**.
channel	To spell cha**nn**el, think of C**NN**.
dependent	Take depend**ent**s to the **dent**ist.
descendant	Descend**ant**s come from **an**cestors.
February	**Br**! It's Fe**br**uary.
grammar	Bad gram**mar** will **mar** your writing.
privilege	A privi**leg**e gives you a **leg** up.
recommend	Re**commend** contains the word **commend**.
separate	To sep**ar**ate is to **par**t.
stationery	**Pen**s are for writing on station**e**ry.

Exercise 2   *Noun Usage Review*

Computer Tip

A computer spell checker can't tell whether a word should be possessive or not, so it won't pick up an error if you confuse possessive and plural forms of nouns.

Choose the correct form of each noun in parentheses, and indicate whether it is possessive singular, possessive plural, or just plural (not possessive).

1. Genealogy is the search for a (families, family's, families') roots in the past.

2. Alex (Haley's, Haleys, Haleys') book *Roots*, in which he traced his own ancestry back to Africa, renewed many (people's, peoples, peoples') interest in genealogical research.

3. Sometimes it is difficult to trace past (generation's, generations, generations') because of (change's, changes, changes') in names.

4. Once they have completed their search, many people like to travel to their (ancestors, ancestor's, ancestors') birthplace.

5. The (result's, results, results') of your own research could help you create a chart or family tree, starting with you and branching back to past generations.

6. A chart will show how the number of ancestors increases with each generation back, a fact that seems to be at odds with (historian's, historians, historians') knowledge that the (world's, worlds, worlds') population is a lot larger than it used to be.

7. Scientists have discovered that certain of our (ancestors, ancestor's, ancestors') acted as more than just "one ancestor" in our past; one person could be connected into our ancestry several times.

8. The (chance's, chances, chances') are that nobody in the world—regardless of race—can be any further away from you than your fiftieth cousin!

Sniglets

Sniglets are words that aren't in the dictionary, but should be. For example...

elbonics	*noun.* the actions of two people manoeuvring for one armrest at the theatre
examnesia	*noun.* forgetting everything as soon as an exam starts
wondracide	*noun.* the act of murdering a piece of fresh bread with cold butter and a knife
retrocarbonic	*adjective.* any soft drink machine that dispenses the drink before the cup
subnougate	*verb.* to eat the bottom caramels in a box of candy and replace the top level, hoping no one will notice
frust	*noun.* small line of dust that eludes dustpan
rignition	*noun.* starting the engine when the car is already running
fuzztache	*noun.* moustache of a teenager before he starts to shave

Can you suggest any other sniglets?

Using Pronouns

A pronoun is a word that is used in place of a noun or another pronoun.

The word to which a pronoun refers is its antecedent.

> Deep in the woods, a dove was singing *its* sad song.
> (The pronoun *its* refers to the noun *dove*. *Dove* is the antecedent of *its*.)

> Ralph and Anna fixed the airplane's engine using *her* pliers.
> (The pronoun *her* refers to *Anna*, who owns the pliers. *Anna* is the antecedent of *her*.)

Latin Roots

Pronoun *comes from the Latin word* pro, *meaning* for, *and* nomen *meaning* name.

Pronoun Usage

One of the reasons why it's important for you to learn how to use pronouns correctly is that they are used so often. For example, the preceding sentence itself contains four pronouns. Can you find them?

There are only a few situations in which pronouns are particularly confusing. By mastering these, you can avoid the problems that many people have in using pronouns.

Classes of Pronouns

A class is a group of similar things. Pronouns can be divided into a number of different classes, as shown in the following chart.

Classes of Pronouns

Personal

I, you, he, she, it, we, they, me, her, him, us, them, my, mine, your, yours, hers, his, its, our, ours, their, theirs

Reflexive

myself, yourself, himself, herself, itself, ourselves, yourselves, themselves

Demonstrative

this, that, these, those

Interrogative

who, whose, whom, which, what

Relative

who, whose, whom, which, what, that

Indefinite

all, another, any, anybody, anyone, anything, both, each, either, everybody, everyone, everything, few, many, more, most, much, neither, nobody, none, no one, nothing, one, other, several, such, some, somebody, someone, something

The Practical Pronoun

Here are two sentences that say the same thing, the first without and the second with pronouns.

Jane and Jane's mother got Jane's brother's jacket repaired before Jane's brother knew that the jacket's zipper was broken.

Jane and her mother got her brother's jacket repaired before he knew that its zipper was broken.

Personal Pronouns

Personal pronouns take their name from the fact that most of them are used to refer to persons. There are three forms, or **cases**, of personal pronouns. Use the **nominative** form (*I, you, he,* etc.) as the subject of a verb; the **objective** form (*me, him, her,* etc.) as the direct or indirect object; and the **possessive** form (*mine, his, hers,* etc.) to indicate ownership or possession.

Objects

*A **direct object** tells who or what receives the action of the verb. An **indirect object** tells to whom or to what about the verb. In the sentence,* I gave the spinach leaf to Isaac, *the direct object is* the spinach leaf (*gave what?) and the indirect object is* Isaac (*gave to whom?).*

Forms of Personal Pronouns			
	Nominative	Objective	Possessive
Singular	I	me	my, mine
	you	you	your, yours
	she, he, it	her, him, it	her, hers, his, its
Plural	we	us	our, ours
	you	you	your, yours
	they	them	their, theirs

How do you know whether to use a possessive, an objective, or a nominative pronoun? Just ask yourself, How will the pronoun be used? If it will be used to show ownership or belonging, a possessive pronoun is correct. If it will be used as an object, an objective pronoun is correct. If it will be used as a subject or predicate pronoun, a nominative pronoun is correct.

You probably use personal pronouns correctly most of the time. However, there are a few situations in which personal pronouns can cause problems. These are described below.

Personal Pronouns after the Verb *To Be*

After a form of the verb *to be*, such as *is, was, will be,* or *has been*, always use a nominative pronoun.

> It was *they* who flew the first shuttle mission.
> The student directors will be Mac and *she*.

To tell which pronoun to use, try reversing the subject and the pronoun. The reversed sentence should still make sense. *Them flew the first shuttle mission* doesn't sound right, and it isn't.

Personal Pronouns in Compounds

Sometimes two pronouns, or a pronoun and a noun, are joined by *and*, *or*, or *nor* to form a compound. Remember, the way a pronoun is used always determines its form. In a compound, use the same form of the pronoun that you would use if the pronoun appeared by itself.

> *Nick and I* baked baklava for the Greek holiday. (*I* baked baklava...)
>
> The darkness closed in on *Marco and me*. (...closed in on *me*.)
>
> The team members that day were *Boris and I*. (The team member was *I*.)
>
> Dad took *Maria and me* to the movies. (Dad took *me*...)

Between Friends

In informal speech between friends, it's common for people to use objective pronouns after the verb to be, *as in* I'm her *or* It is me. *However, in formal speech and writing, retain the proper nominative forms, as in* I'm she *or* It is I.

Quick Tip

To tell which pronoun to use in a compound, try the pronoun by itself, without the other part of the compound. "The darkness closed in on I" sounds odd and is incorrect.

We and *Us* Before Nouns

Sometimes the pronouns *we* and *us* are used as modifiers before nouns. If the modified noun is a subject or predicate noun, use *we*. If the noun is an object, use *us*.

Incorrect   *Us* windsurfers love the sun.
              (Windsurfers is the subject of the verb *love*. Therefore, you need to use *we*.)

Correct   *We* windsurfers love the sun.

Incorrect   However, the sun can give *we* windsurfers terrible burns.
              (Windsurfers is the object of the verb *give*. Therefore, you need to use *us*.)

Correct   However, the sun can give *us* windsurfers terrible burns.

Quick Tip

To determine which pronoun to use, try using the pronoun by itself. "The sun can give *we* terrible burns" sounds odd. "The sun can give *us* terrible burns" sounds right, and it is.

Choose the correct pronoun from those in parentheses.

1. (We, Us) Canadians don't go in much for heroes, but Silken Laumann certainly gained that status as an Olympic athlete.

2. It was (her, she) who came back from a terrible leg injury to win a bronze medal in rowing.

3. Laumann was badly injured just ten weeks before the Olympics when her scull collided with another boat rowed by two Germans; she and (them, they) were both taken to hospital.

4. Between you and (me, I), when I heard that she was going to try to make the Olympics anyway, I thought she was crazy.

5. Richard Backus thought so, too; it was (he, him) who treated Silken's leg after the accident.

6. The injury forced Laumann and (he, him) to alter her training schedule—but not for very long.

7. Neither you nor (me, I) nor anyone else can imagine the amount of effort she must have made to get back to her pre-accident training schedule in just six short weeks.

8. Laumann's efforts gave (we, us) Canadians something to cheer about that summer.

9. Nothing was more important to (she, her) and her teammates than competing in the Olympics.

10. And although someone else was wearing the gold medal, the real winner on that podium was (she, her).

Using *Who* and *Whom*

Use *who* and *whom* exactly as you use personal pronouns. *Who* is a nominative pronoun. It is used as a subject or as a predicate pronoun. *Whom* is an objective pronoun. It is used as an object.

Subject	*Who* designed the first hot-air balloon?
Predicate Pronoun	The designers were *who*?
Direct Object	*Whom* did the first balloon carry?
Object of a Preposition	By *whom* was the first balloon flown?

Who and *whom* are often used in questions. They also appear as part of longer statements, like this one:

> He is the architect (who, whom) designed the
> National Gallery.

To determine which pronoun to use, isolate the group of words to which the pronoun belongs, and substitute *he* or *him* for the missing pronoun. If *he* sounds right, use *who.* If *him* sounds right, use *whom.*

> (who, whom) designed the National Gallery.
> *He* designed the National Gallery. (Since *he* sounds
> right, *who* is correct.)
> He is the architect *who* designed the National Gallery.

Quick Tip

Since *him* and *whom* both have the letter *m* in them, it is easy to remember that they are both in the same (objective) case.

Exercise 2   Who *and* Whom

Choose the correct pronoun from those given in parentheses.

1. Birute Galdikas is a Canadian woman (who, whom) spends eight months of every year living with the orangutans in the Indonesian rain forest.

2. Galdikas is one of three women (who, whom) the famous anthropologist Louis Leakey picked to conduct long-term studies of primates in their natural habitats.

3. The other two researchers are Jane Goodall, (who, whom) is famous for her work with chimpanzees, and Dian Fossey, (who, whom) poachers murdered in 1985 because of her battle to save the gorillas.

4. In the twenty-odd years since she first arrived in Indonesia, Galdikas has made many discoveries about the life of the orangutans, (who, whom) are highly intelligent.

5. No modern scientist had ever seen two male orangutans fight each other until Galdikas, (who, whom) had to wait patiently for months before witnessing the event.

6. Orangutans, (who, whom) live high in the tree canopy of the dense rain forest, are particularly hard to study.

Uses of Who and Whom

Who *and* whom *are sometimes used as interrogative pronouns, to ask questions.*

Who *was that?*

Sometimes they are used to introduce subordinate clauses. A **subordinate clause** *is a group of words with a subject and a verb that cannot stand on its own as a sentence.*

She was the performer who *revolutionized rock music.*

7. Galdikas and the research team with (who, whom) she works spend their days tracking the apes through leech-infested swamps.

8. Yet Galdikas, (who, whom) claims she was born to do this work, has never thought of quitting.

9. Like Goodall and Fossey, Galdikas has fought to preserve the remaining habitat of the apes (who, whom) she studies.

10. Indonesian forestry officials, (who, whom) see the rain forest as a source of logging revenues, tried to cancel her research permit; but Galdikas fought back and won the right to stay, at least for a while.

Euphemisms

Dysphemisms

Dysphemisms are just the opposite of euphemisms: they are vulgar, coarse, or ugly expressions, such as croak *for* die; plastered *for* drunk; *and* slammer *for* jail.

Euphemisms (pronounced U-phe-misms) are words or phrases that name things in an indirect or mild way because the direct way is perceived as unpleasant or harsh. Euphemisms can be good or bad, sensible or silly:

laid to rest	buried
correctional institution	prison
misleading phrase	lie
preowned, reconditioned	used
passed away	died

Some of the above euphemisms could be used for the sake of kindness; others are plainly designed to hide the truth. Be aware of the distinction. Most writers try to avoid using euphemisms. It is usually better to use the simpler term.

Advertisements are one of the best sources of euphemisms. Listen closely to the ads on television, and see how many euphemisms you can collect for the following terms:

Example **small size** personal size, travel size, pocket size

large size   **soap**   **hair dye**   **car**

QUIZ: Can you tell what these euphemisms are referring to?

starter home   military solution
golden age endowment   leather-like

Answers
small house, old age pension, war, vinyl

Reflexive Pronouns

Use reflexive pronouns only when they have an antecedent in the same sentence.

When a reflexive pronoun appears in a sentence, the word that it refers to—its antecedent—must appear in the same sentence.

> Emile sent himself a love letter.
> (Emile is the antecedent of *himself*.)

Never use one of these pronouns without an antecedent.

Incorrect   Atiya and *myself* built the set.
          (*Myself* does not refer to another word in the sentence.)
Correct   Atiya and I built the set.

Reflexive Pronouns
Reflexive pronouns are created by adding -self *or* -selves *to certain personal pronouns:*
Singular *myself, yourself, himself, herself, itself*
Plural *ourselves, yourselves, themselves*
Note that the list does not include hisself *and* theirselves. *They are nonstandard.*

Exercise 3   *Reflexive Pronouns*

Rewrite the following sentences, replacing the blanks with an appropriate personal or reflexive pronoun.

1. In the eleventh century, a Chinese astrologer named Yan Wei-Te prostrated _____ before his emperor to share an amazing discovery.

2. The emperor and _____ marvelled at his discovery, a new star in the heavens.

3. You and _____ now know that the new "star" was actually the supernova known as the Crab Nebula.

4. A supernova occurs when a star explodes and collapses in on _____; the glow from the explosion can be seen across the universe.

5. The Crab Nebula _____ is sixty-five hundred light years from Earth, in the constellation Taurus.

6. Recently, a professor found _____ wondering about the design on an ancient Native American bowl he was examining.

7. He noticed that _____ contained a picture of a rabbit kicking a twenty-three pointed star.

8. The appearance of a star was not the only coincidence; the number of points was _____ significant because the Chinese had said that the Crab Nebula appeared for twenty-three days.

9. Archaeologists, who study ancient societies, date the bowl to the eleventh century, which is when the supernova _____ appeared.

10. Although he didn't know it _____, that Chinese astrologer may very well have had a fellow stargazer in North America.

Indefinite Pronouns

An indefinite pronoun is one that does not refer to a definite person or thing. Some indefinite pronouns are singular, some are plural, and some can be singular or plural, depending on their use.

Singular	another, either, neither, anybody, everybody, nobody, somebody, anyone, everyone, no one, someone, anything, everything, nothing, something, each, much
Plural	few, many, several
Singular or Plural	all, enough, most, plenty, any, more, none, some, other(s), one(s)

Singular   *Most* of the lake was dried up.
(*Most* refers to the singular word *lake*. Therefore, it is singular and takes a singular verb, *was*.)

Plural   *Most* of the lakes in the area are low.
(*Most* refers to the plural word *lakes*. Therefore, it is plural and takes a plural verb, *are*.)

Quick Tip

Don't be confused by a prepositional phrase between the subject and the verb. A verb never agrees with a word in a prepositional phrase.

When a personal pronoun refers to an indefinite pronoun, the two pronouns must agree.

> *Anyone* who wants to join a girls' softball team should sign *her* name on the list in the hall.
> (*Anyone* is singular, so the pronoun that refers to it should also be singular.)

Quick Tip

The phrase "his or her" is singular and can be used in place of *his* or *her* alone when the **gender**, or sex, of the person referred to is not known.

Exercise 4   *Indefinite Pronouns*

Rewrite the following sentences, inserting the correct pronouns.

1. In the winter many humpback whales gather near Hawaii to bear (her, their) young.

2. In the spring, each of them (travel, travels) thousands of kilometres in search of (his or her, their) feeding ground.

3. Some of them end (his or her, their) journey on the California coast.

4. Others continue on (his or her, their) way up as far as Northern Canada and Alaska.

5. Each of the whales seems to return to (his or her, their) same feeding ground year after year.

6. Everyone in the scientific community has (their, his or her) own opinion about how whales choose a feeding ground.

7. One of the scientists who has published (his, their) research into this question took a substance called DNA from the whales.

8. He found that all of the whales (choose, chooses) the same feeding ground that (their, his or her) mothers choose.

9. None of the scientists (has, have) convinced (himself or herself, themselves) as to the scientific reasons for this.

10. Perhaps many in the whale community love (his or her, their) mothers.

Reminder

*The **gender** of a pronoun can be male* (he), *female* (she), *or neuter* (it). *Note that plural pronouns can refer to either males or females* (they, their, them).

Other Problems with Pronouns

Ambiguous Pronoun Reference

A word or a phrase is **ambiguous** if it can be taken more than one way. You should always be able to tell what word a pronoun refers to. If you can't—if the pronoun could refer as easily to one word as to another—then you need to rewrite the sentence to make it clear to what the pronoun refers.

Unclear   The jeweller took the stone out of the setting and examined *it*. (Does the pronoun *it* refer to *setting* or to *stone*?)

Clear   After removing the stone, the jeweller examined *its* setting.

OR

Clear   The jeweller removed the stone and examined *it*.

Indefinite Antecedent

As you know, the antecedent is the word to which a pronoun refers. A reader or listener should always be able to tell what the antecedent of a pronoun is.

Unclear   The movie director wasn't happy, but she said *it* could be redone. (What was the director unhappy about? To what does the pronoun *it* refer? The antecedent is unclear.)

Clear   The movie director wasn't happy with the shot, but she said *it* could be redone.

Pronouns and Gender

The English language does not have a neutral singular pronoun to refer to both men and women. In the past, it was acceptable to use the male pronouns (*he, him, his*) to refer to human beings in general. However, this is no longer acceptable in most general situations. Here are some ideas to help you avoid the gender problem.

Create Your Own Pronoun!

Many words have been suggested as replacements for the phrase "his or her," including tey, co, E, ne, thon, mon, heesh, ho, hesh, et, hir, jhe, na, per, xe, po, and person. None of these forms has really caught on, however. Can you think of any possible replacements?

- Use *he or she, him or her*, or *his or her* in place of *he, him*, or *his* when the sex of the person referred to is unknown or irrelevant.

  These phrases are considered to be singular, so they can be used with singular indefinite pronouns.

  > Everyone is responsible for his or her own belongings.

  Unfortunately, too many of these phrases together can sound awkward. Try not to overuse this method.

- Change the sentence from singular to plural.

  Since the plural personal pronouns can be used for both men and women, you can avoid the issue altogether by switching to the plural.

  Sexist: A doctor should treat his patients with respect.
  Non-Sexist: Doctors should treat their patients with respect.

- Replace the male pronoun with *you* or *one*.

  Sexist: A job applicant has to sell himself to his potential employer.

  Non-Sexist: When you apply for a job, you have to sell yourself to your potential employer.
  Non-Sexist: When applying for a job, one must sell oneself to the potential employer.

- Reword the sentence to eliminate all male and female pronouns.

  Sexist: You can tell a lot about someone by the clothes he wears.
  Non-Sexist: Clothes reveal a lot about a person.

The Politics of Pronouns

In informal speech, it is becoming acceptable to use a plural pronoun to refer to a singular indefinite pronoun:

Whoever takes on the task will need to have all their wits about them.

However, it is not yet acceptable to use this construction in written English.

You or One?

Use one *as a replacement in formal writing, and* you *in more casual works.*

Non-Sexist Language

Instead of...	Try...
man, mankind	human, humans, human beings, humanity, humankind, the human race, people, civilization
to man (verb)	to operate, run, staff, attend, drive, use, work
manmade	fabricated, artificial, manufactured, synthetic
manpower	labour, human resources, personnel, staff, work force
businessman	executive, entrepreneur, manager
craftsman	artisan
fireman	firefighter
policeman	police officer
salesman	sales representative, sales clerk
spokesman	spokesperson, speaker, representative, official
sportsman	athlete, competitor, player
workman	worker, employee

Can you think of a non-sexist version for the second line of *O Canada*? (Remember, it has to be easy to sing!)

> O Canada! Our home and native land
> True patriot love in all thy sons command.

Pronouns and Contractions

A **contraction** is formed when two words are joined together in a special way. One or more of the letters in the second word are replaced by an apostrophe. These are some of the most common contractions:

it's = it + is	they're = they + are
you're = you + are	who's = who + is

Do not confuse these contractions with the possessive pronouns *its*, *their*, *your*, and *whose*.

Incorrect *Whose* going to show me how to use this computer?

Correct *Who's* going to show me how to use this computer?

To decide whether a contraction is correct in a sentence, substitute the words for which the contraction stands. In the example above, "Who is going to show me" sounds correct and is.

Exercise 5   *Other Pronoun Problems*

Choose the correct word from those in parentheses for each of the following sentences. Then rewrite the paragraph, eliminating the repetition of *he or she*, *him or her*, and *his or her*.

1. (Your, You're) body language can send out strong signals to others, even when (your, you're) not aware of it.

2. "Tongue showing" is one of those signals; anyone (whose, who's) sticking out the tip of (his or her, their) tongue is sending the signal, "Don't bother me, I'm busy."

3. A child (whose, who's) concentrating very hard on some task is likely to have his or her tongue sticking out.

4. Adults also show their tongues to warn people off, but curiously, we're often unaware (its, it's) showing.

5. Even more curiously, a person (whose, who's) received (them, those) tongue-showing signals will likely think twice before disturbing you, but he or she won't know what made him or her so cautious!

Exercise 6   *Pronoun Usage Review*

Rewrite the following sentences, inserting the correct pronoun.

1. (We, Us) teenagers just love classic horror movies.

2. My sister and (I, myself) have seen Boris Karloff as Frankenstein at least twenty times!

3. Will you come to the theatre with Lindsay and (I, me) next time we go to see *Frankenstein*?

4. Boris Karloff played Frankenstein, and it was also (he, him) who played the lead in the 1932 film called *The Mummy*.

5. His voice could make me run out of the theatre, but I've heard that he (himself, hisself) was a very kind man.

6. Another actor (whose, who's) voice was captivating was Vincent Price.

7. Bette Davis, (who, whom) had already won two Academy Awards, starred in a series of macabre films in the 1960s.

8. It was (she, her) who played opposite Joan Crawford in *Whatever Happened to Baby Jane?*

9. With (who, whom) do you like to cook up a batch of popcorn, turn down the lights, and be consumed by fright?

Homonyms

They're, their, and there *are* **homonyms**—*words that sound alike but mean different things. Here are some more triple homonyms:*
buy/by/bye
sees/seas/seize
write/right/rite
flew/flu/flue
two/too/to
four/fore/for
oar/ore/or
sight/site/cite
rays/raise/raze
rain/reign/rein
vein/vain/vane
sow/so/sew

Using Modifiers

Modifiers are words that change or limit the meaning of other words. Two kinds of modifiers are adjectives and adverbs.

Adjectives

An adjective is a word that modifies a noun or a pronoun.

An adjective answers one of these questions: Which one? What kind? How many? How much?

>   *this* horn, *pine* tree, *several* days, *fewer* books

Classes of Adjectives

Articles   *A*, *an*, and *the* are adjectives referred to as articles. The article *the* is the **definite article** because it points out a specific person, place, thing, or group.

A and *an* are **indefinite articles** because they do not refer to specific items. Use *an* before a vowel sound. Use *a* before a consonant sound. Remember, it is the sound, not the spelling, that determines the correct choice: *an* ear, *an* heir, *an* oboe, *a* house.

Proper Adjectives   These are adjectives formed from proper nouns and are always capitalized: *Italian* ice, *Napoleonic* wars.

Predicate Adjectives   These adjectives follow linking verbs and describe the subject of the sentence: Her feet are *cold*. The room looks *peaceful*.

Nouns as Adjectives   Nouns become modifiers when they describe nouns: *blood* pressure, *rock* garden, *infant* seat.

Adverbs

An adverb modifies a verb, an adjective, or another adverb.

Modifies Verb   demonstrated *angrily*, plays *well*

Modifies Adjective *too* difficult, *moderately* helpful

Modifies Adverb   *so* simply, *quite* often

Adverbs tell *where, when, how,* or *to what extent* about the words they modify.

How   smiled *mockingly*, ran *fast*

Where   went *there*, fell *down*

When   begins *soon*, *always* works

To What Extent   *completely* honest, *partially* finished

Many adverbs are formed by adding *-ly* to an adjective.

bright + *-ly* = brightly   merry + *-ly* = merrily

Commonly Used Adverbs That Do Not End in -ly

afterward	even	long	often	today
almost	far	low	seldom	tomorow
already	fast	more	soon	too
also	forth	never	still	well
away	here	next	straight	yesterday
back	instead	not	then	yet
before	late	now	there	

Adjective or Adverb?

Adjectives and adverbs help you create strong, lively images. Knowing a few guidelines will help you use them properly. If you can't decide whether to use an adjective or an adverb in a sentence, ask yourself the following questions:

1. Which word does the modifier describe? Use an adverb if the modified word is an action verb, adjective, or adverb. Use an adjective if the modified word is a noun or pronoun.

2. What does the modifier tell about the word it describes?
   Use an adverb if the modifier tells *how, when, where,* or *to what extent.* Use an adjective if the modifier tells *which one, what kind, how many,* or *how much.*

   > She was (real, really) upset about the change of plans.
   > (The adverb *really* is the correct choice because the modifier describes the adjective *upset.*)

Exercise 1   *Adjective or Adverb?*

Choose the correct modifier from the two in parentheses. Then write the word or words it modifies and whether the modifier is an adjective or an adverb.

Example   The train raced (quick, quickly) toward its
             destination.
Answer   quickly / raced / adverb

1. A city like Rome offers (extraordinary, extraordinarily) evidence of the talent and suffering of human beings.

2. The Caesars, who ruled Rome in its early days, worked (tireless, tirelessly) to create a vast empire.

3. During that time great artists designed the city's (fabulous, fabulously) temples, palaces, monuments, and fountains.

4. Most citizens lived in (miserable, miserably) conditions.

5. The rulers (cleverly, clever) provided free food and entertainment to Rome's residents, hoping that "bread and circuses" would calm the desperate citizens.

6. This ancient city was built (large, largely) by human slavery and suffering.

7. Every third person in Caesar's Rome suffered (deep, deeply) as a slave.

8. In the summer of A.D. 64, a fire raged (uncontrollable, uncontrollably) throughout the city for ten days.

9. Rome was destroyed (frequent, frequently) by natural disasters including floods, earthquakes, and plagues.

10. Despite Rome's history of disasters and wars, it has survived (magnificently, magnificent) as one of the world's greatest cities.

Latin Prefixes

Prefixes are groups of letters that are added to the beginning of other words to change their meaning. If you can recognize a prefix on a word, you have a clue to its meaning. Many English prefixes come from Latin, the language spoken in ancient Rome.

Think of at least one more word to add to each of the following lists.

ab	from (absent, abject, abrogate...)
ad	toward (adjective, address...)
ante	before (antecedent, antechamber, antedate...)
contra	against (contradict, contrast, contralto...)
cum/con	with (confer, communicate, condescend...)
extra	outside (extramural, extraterrestrial, extraordinary...)
inter	between (interaction, interjection, interest...)
per	through (perambulate, perform, pertain...)
post	after (postscript, postoperative, postpartum, postgraduate...)
pro	for (project, provide, protect, product...)
sub	below (subterranean, submarine, subsume, subject...)
super	above (superman, supercilious, superstitious...)
trans	across (transcontinental, transit, transitive...)
uni	one (unanimous, unity, unison, unicycle...)

Spelling

Sometimes when a prefix is joined to a word, the spelling of the prefix (or the word) is changed slightly.

cum (with)
+ langere (to touch)
= contact

Adverb or Predicate Adjective?

Use an adverb to modify an action verb. Use an adjective after a linking verb.

Most verbs are action verbs and so can be modified by adverbs. Linking verbs, such as *be* or *seem*, however, don't usually take modifiers. They are often followed by an adjective, which actually modifies the subject, not the verb. An adjective used in this way is called a **predicate adjective**.

The dress is *elegant*.
(*Elegant* is a predicate adjective modifying *dress*.)

The men seemed *angry*.
(*Angry* is a predicate adjective modifying *men*.)

Verbs like *appear, look, sound, feel, taste, grow,* and *smell* can be used either as action verbs or as linking verbs. An action verb is modified by an adverb. A linking verb connects a subject with an adjective that describes the subject. For help in deciding whether to use an adjective or an adverb, think about which word will be modified. Use an adjective to modify the subject. Use an adverb to modify the verb.

> The horse looked *nervously* at the jockey.
> (The adverb *nervously* modifies the action verb *looked*.)

> The horse looked *nervous* before the race.
> (The predicate adjective *nervous* modifies the subject, *horse*, not the linking verb *looked*.)

If you are uncertain about whether to use an adverb or an adjective after a verb like *feel, sound, smell,* or *look,* ask yourself the following questions:

1. Can you substitute *is* or *was* for the verb? If you can, use an adjective.
   The coin *appeared* rare. The coin *is* rare.
2. Does the modifier tell *how, when, where,* or *to what extent* about an action verb? If it does, use an adverb.
   This coin *rarely* appears at coin auctions.

Painting with Words

"Often while reading a book one feels that the author would have preferred to paint rather than write; one can sense the pleasure he derives from describing a landscape or a person, as if he were painting what he is saying, because deep in his heart he would have preferred to use brushes and colours."

Pablo Picasso

Exercise 2   *Adverb or Predicate Adjective?*

Choose the correct modifier for each of the following sentences.

1. Maki looked (quick, quickly) around the museum.
2. She seemed (careful, carefully) about following the museum's map.
3. Maki saw Henri Matisse's cutouts (sudden, suddenly) as she entered the room.
4. The giant murals looked (magnificent, magnificently) on the museum walls.
5. The bright colours contrasted (dramatic, dramatically) with the white walls.
6. Maki (quick, quickly) read the notes about Matisse's cutouts.
7. The artist felt (weak, weakly) toward the end of his life.
8. He was (fearful, fearfully) about losing his ability to paint.
9. Matisse began to "draw" with scissors; his giant cutouts expressed his feelings (wonderful, wonderfully).
10. These spectacular cutouts suggest the (perfect, perfectly) combination of all five sensations—taste, smell, touch, sight, and sound.

Malapropisms and Spoonerisms

Malapropisms are named for a character called Mrs. Malaprop in Richard Sheridan's play, *The Rivals*, who often used the wrong word, with amusing results. Can you tell what word the malapropic speaker meant to use in each of these sentences? Answers are below.

Tell me all the perpendiculars.
This movie is not for the screamish.
The first thing they do when a baby is born is cut the biblical cord.
I ate in a restaurant today where the food was abdominal.
Senators are chosen as committee chairs on the basis of senility.

Spoonerisms are named for W.A. Spooner (1844-1930), an English clergyman and professor who often mixed up the first letters of words. For example, he once said "tearful chidings" instead of "cheerful tidings"! Try deciphering the mixed-up meanings of the following phrases. The answers are below.

nosey little cook
a scoop of Boy Trouts
a well-boiled icicle
hush my brat
oderarm deundcrant
a fog as thick as sea poop
have a cough of cuppee

A Spooner Original

Dr. Spooner is reported to have told one of his students, "You have hissed all my mystery lectures and tasted a whole worm."

Answers
Malapropisms: particulars, squeamish, umbilical, abominable, seniority
Spoonerisms: cozy little nook, a troop of Boy Scouts, a well-oiled bicycle, brush my hat, underarm deodorant, a fog as thick as pea soup, have a cup of coffee

Phrases as Modifiers

You have already learned about single-word modifiers. Groups of words can also modify. A **phrase** is a group of related words that does not contain a verb. Phrases cannot stand alone; they always occur as part of a longer sentence. There are three types of phrases that can be used as modifiers.

1. **Prepositional phrases** consist of a preposition, its object, and any modifiers. Prepositional phrases function either as adjectives or as adverbs in a sentence.

   Adjective Prepositional Phrase:

   prep   object of prep

   The town *on the mountain* is Invermere.

   Adverb Prepositional Phrase:

   prep object of prep.

   She worked *before lunch*.

Prepositional Poetry

How many prepositional phrases can you find in this poem?

First Political Speech

first, in the first place, to begin with, secondly,
in the second place, lastly

again, also, in the next space, once more, moreover,
furthermore, likewise, besides, similarly, for example,
for instance, another

then, nevertheless, still, however, at the same time,
yet, in spite of that, on the other hand, on the contrary,
certainly, surely, doubtless, indeed, perhaps, possibly,
probably, anyway, in all probability, in all likelihood,
at all events, in any case

therefore, consequently, accordingly, thus, as a result,
in consequence of this, as might be expected

the foregoing, the preceding, as previously mentioned

as already stated

Eli Mandel

2. **Verbal Phrases** begin with a participle or an infinitive of a verb. A **participle** is a verb that ends in *-ing, -en, -t,* or *-ed.* A participial phrase is often set off from the main sentence by a comma or commas. It almost always functions as an adjective.

    > *Wading through the muskeg*, he wondered why it was there.

    > Nellie McClung, *remembered for her devotion to human rights*, was the author of sixteen books.

    > *Bent in two*, the fork was useless.

3. The infinitive is the dictionary form of the verb with *to* in front of it. **Infinitive phrases** can function as nouns, adjectives, or adverbs.

    Noun   I hate *to cook.*
    Adjective She is the woman *to ask.*
    Adverb   The tango is hard *to master.*

> **Reminder**
>
> *Verbals are verb forms that don't act as the verb of a clause or sentence. Instead, they function as adjectives, adverbs, or nouns.*

Exercise 3   *Phrases as Modifiers*

Tell whether each of the underlined phrases is a prepositional phrase, a participial phrase, or an infinitive phrase. Then indicate whether each phrase is functioning as an adjective, adverb, or noun.

APRIL 13: east of Lagartos, Mexico
We decided <u>to try to paddle</u> at night while the winds were down.

It seems that our last days on the Gulf will be won only if we can gather all our fighting resources and outwit these phenomenal winds. By two o'clock last night, we had paddled 11 km.

Then the moon went down, <u>throwing our world into impenetrable darkness</u>. I couldn't even see Dana's outline ahead of me <u>in the canoe</u>.

By four o'clock we'd grown so weary we were dozing off as we paddled. I'd drift off, <u>awakening to Dana's sharp rebukes</u> — "Do you wanta die? Do you wanta kill us both?" It wasn't long before both of us were in a semi-coma, <u>thoroughly disoriented, and thoroughly lost</u>.

> **Source Note**
>
> *This excerpt is taken from* Paddle to the Amazon *by Don Starkell. Starkell tells the story of his two-year, twenty-thousand-kilometre canoe trip from Winnipeg to the Amazon River with his teenage son, Dana.*

<u>At about five</u> in the morning I had begun <u>to hallucinate</u>. I now saw rock cliffs, then a wall of palms. At one point, unable to stand it, I laid my head back on the stern deck, but was soon jolted upright by Dana's frenzied shouting. Back and forth we zigzagged — asleep, awake, asleep again.

<u>After six hours of torment</u>, the first hint of dawn appeared ahead.

Modifiers in Comparisons

Comparing people, things, and actions is part of everyday life. You might say, for example:

> "The Oilers are a better team than the Leafs. Their defence is better, and they have faster skaters." Or you might say, "The Oilers skate quickly, but the Leafs skate more quickly."

In comparisons, modifiers have special forms or spellings.

The Comparative

When you compare one person, thing, or action with another, use the **comparative** form of the modifier.

> China is *larger* than Japan.
> Samantha runs *faster* than Bai.

The comparative form is generally made in two ways:

1. **For short modifiers add *-er*.**

   cold + -er = colder   thin + er = thinner

   juicy + -er = juicier   bold + -er = bolder

2. **For longer modifiers use *more*.**

   more interesting   more beautiful

   Most modifiers ending in *-ful* or *-ous* form the comparative with *more*.

   more fearful   more anxious

> ### Reminder
>
> *Some modifiers cannot form comparisons. For example, something that is unique is one of a kind. It cannot be more or less unique than something else. Some other modifiers that cannot form comparisons are* equal, fatal, favourite, final, different, *and* absolute.

> Most two-syllable modifiers form the comparative with *-er*. However, a word like *softly* uses *more*. You can usually tell which form to use because the correct form will sound better. For example, you wouldn't say *softlier*.

Six Steps to Better Sentences

1. **Keep them short.** Most magazine sentences average about 16 words.

2. **Keep them simple.** Say what you have to say as straightforwardly as possible.

3. **Avoid unnecessary words.** Make every word count. Don't smother your ideas by using too many modifiers.

4. **Use active verbs.** Avoid the passive voice as much as possible. Verbs add verve.

5. **Use concrete words.** Too many abstract nouns weigh your writing down. Try to use images that appeal to the senses: sight, hearing, touch, smell, and taste.

6. **Vary your sentence patterns.** Be aware of the rhythm of your writing. Keep the reader's attention by varying the length and structure of your sentences.

The Superlative

Whenever you compare a person, thing, or action with more than one other person, thing, or action, use the **superlative** form of the modifier.

> Karl is the *shyest* musician in the band.
>
> Sylvie runs *most energetically* in the morning.

The superlative form of modifiers is generally made by adding *-est* (for short modifiers) or by using *most* (for longer modifiers). For modifiers that take *-er* in the comparative, add *-est* for the superlative. Those words that use *more* to form the comparative use *most* for the superlative.

Double Comparisons

Never use -er and more, *or -est and* most *at the same time. When you use both, the result is called a **double comparison**.*

Double Comparison
Wood is more stronger than plastic.

Correct
Wood is stronger than plastic.

Many people use the superlative incorrectly to compare two things. Consider the following examples:

Incorrect She's the *fastest* of the two swimmers.

Correct She's the *faster* of the two swimmers.

Modifier	Comparative	Superlative
smooth	smoother	smoothest
cute	cuter	cutest
loud	louder	loudest
intricate	more intricate	most intricate
sweetly	more sweetly	most sweetly

 **Quick Tip**

When writing comparisons, always read back over your sentence to make sure the comparison is logical and clear. Sometimes a word missing here or there can make your comparison vague.

Confusing Teresa is better than any player on the team.
(Teresa is good, but she can't be better than herself.)

Clear Teresa is better than any other player on the team.

Confusing Trevor was more afraid of the mouse than the elephant.
(Was Trevor afraid of the mouse and the elephant, or was the elephant afraid of the mouse too?)

Clear Trevor was more afraid of the mouse than the elephant was.

Clear Trevor was more afraid of the mouse than of the elephant.

Irregular Comparisons

Some modifiers make their comparative and superlative forms by complete word changes. The chart on the following page gives some common examples.

Modifier	Comparative	Superlative
good	better	best
well	better	best
bad	worse	worst
little	less or lesser	least
much	more	most
many	more	most
far	farther	farthest

Few and Less

Few (fewer, fewest) *is used for things than can be counted:*

I have a few books to finish reading.

Less (lesser, least) *is used for things that cannot be counted:*

There seems to be less smog this summer than there was last summer.

To make a negative comparison, use *less* or *least* before the modifier: *careful, less careful, least careful.*

Exercise 4   *Review of Comparisons*

Choose the correct modifier from the two in parentheses.

1. My (favourite, most favourite) TV show is *Star Trek: The Next Generation.*

2. I think it is even (funner, more fun) than the original *Star Trek* was.

3. Who would have thought that Gene Roddenberry could have created an even (better, gooder) series than the first?

4. Captain Jean-Luc Picard speaks much (more elegantly, more elegant) than James T. Kirk ever did; that is because he was born in Paris, France.

5. The *Enterprise* itself is (more grand, grander) than the old ship.

6. Most "trekkies" are never (happier, more happier) than when they are watching an episode for the second, third, or even fourth time.

7. I think I will do what Whoopi Goldberg did, and tell the casting director that it would be the (biggest, most big) thrill of my life to appear in a *Star Trek* episode.

8. Goldberg pleaded with the producers to let her act on the show; her character, Guinan, is one of the (most greatest, greatest) on the show.

9. In the original casting descriptions, Worf, the Klingon security officer, did not exist; in his place was to be a tough woman officer called "Macha"; the *Enterprise* without Worf would have been a much less (interesting, interestinger) place.

10. Among TV shows, I think *The Next Generation* is (unique, most unique) in the high quality of its writing, its characters, and its acting.

Special Problems with Modifiers

Some adjectives and adverbs can be especially confusing; in everyday speech you may hear these modifiers used incorrectly. In the following pages you will learn how to avoid some common mistakes.

Them and Those

Them is always a pronoun. It is never used as a modifier. Those is a pronoun when used alone; it is an adjective when followed by a noun.

With *them* and *those*, the most common mistake is using *them* as an adjective. Remember that *them* is always a pronoun; use *those*, not *them*, as a modifier.

Incorrect   What happened to all of *them* elephants?

Correct   What happened to all of *those* elephants?

This and That, These and Those

Use this and that to modify singular nouns. Use these and those to modify plural nouns.

The adjectives *this* and *that* modify singular nouns. *These* and *those* modify plural nouns. When these modifiers are used with words such as *kind, sort,* and *type,* be especially careful to use them correctly.

Incorrect   *Those* kind of apples are delicious.
(*Kind* is singular, so it should be modified by either *this* or *that*.)

Correct   *That* kind of apple is delicious.
(Notice that the noun *apple* and the verb *is* have become singular as well.)

Bad and Badly

Use *bad* as an adjective. Use *badly* as an adverb.

Bad is an adjective, so it should only be used to modify nouns and pronouns. Like other adjectives, *bad* sometimes follows a linking verb. *Badly* is always an adverb, so it should never be used with a linking verb.

Incorrect   He feels *badly* about making us late.
(*Badly* is an adverb that modifies *feels*. This means that the subject is not very good at feeling!)

Correct   He feels *bad* about making us late.

Good and Well

***Good* is an adjective. *Well* is usually an adverb.**

Generally, *good* is used to modify nouns or pronouns. Use *well* to modify verbs, adverbs, and adjectives.

> I did the job *well*.
> She gave a *good* performance.

The only exception to this rule is in matters relating to health. *Well* usually functions as an adverb meaning "expertly" or "properly." But it may also mean "in good health"; when it does, it is an adjective, used after a linking verb.

> After the fever passed, my brother seemed *well*.
> (adjective)
> We cared for him *well* during his recovery. (adverb)

Since *good* and *well* can both be adjectives, they can both be used as predicate adjectives after linking verbs. To decide which word to use in a sentence, remember that *well* refers to health, while *good* refers to happiness, comfort, or pleasure.

> Marek stayed home from school because he didn't feel well.
> Luisa felt good after she saved the rabbit's life.

Exercise 5   *Problem Modifiers*

Choose the correct modifier from those in parentheses.

1.   Sandra and her family took a trip to see the spectacular art of the Haida; their ten-year-old jalopy ran (well, good) throughout the journey.

2. Sandra's brother, Jonas, had been ill and was not (good, well) enough to join them on the trip.

3. Sandra felt (bad, badly) that her brother had to stay home.

4. It wasn't until they reached their destination that Sandra started to feel (good, well) about the trip.

5. At a totem pole exhibit, Sandra said, "The brochure claims that (this, these) kind of Native art almost died out around the turn of the century, when Native people stopped carving the poles."

6. "Mortuary poles were carved to honour the dead, while memorial poles were reserved for chiefs; (this, these) kinds of poles are less common than house pillars, which were the earliest kind of totem."

7. Sandra also learned that (that, those) species of animals carved on the poles told a story, but that it was almost impossible to tell what the story was unless you were present when the pole was raised.

8. Totems were usually raised at potlatches, ceremonies in which clans showed each other how (well, good) they were doing by lavishing gifts on their guests, who later returned the favour.

9. At a Native gift shop, Sandra and her mother saw lots of (them, those) kinds of woven baskets that the Haida make.

10. "I think Jonas will like (this, these) kind of argillite carving," said Sandra, as she bought a small statue for her brother.

The Double Negative

Do not use two negatives together.

The most common negative words are *no, not, never, nothing,* and *none*. Sometimes you will hear people use two negative words together, especially with a contraction such as *didn't* or *couldn't*. This kind of error is called a **double negative**.

Incorrect Shaheen couldn't find no scissors in the closet.

Correct Shaheen couldn't find any scissors in the closet.

Correct Shaheen could find no scissors in the closet.

Remember that the *-n't* in a contraction means "not." If you pair a contraction containing *-n't* with another negative word, you end up with a double negative.

Hardly, barely, never, and *scarcely* are often used as negative words. Do not use them after contractions like *haven't* or *couldn't*.

Incorrect The children *couldn't barely* hear the music.

Correct The children *could* barely hear the music.

Exercise 6   *Double Negatives*

Rewrite the following sentences, using the negative word in parentheses and avoiding a double negative.

Example   We couldn't ask him to carry all the camping gear. (hardly)

Answer   We could hardly ask him to carry all the camping gear.

(Incorrect: We couldn't hardly ask him to carry all the camping gear.)

1. When she was young, the Barry girl wasn't interested in anything but medicine. (nothing)

2. Unfortunately, in the early 1800s it was impossible for women to study at university. (not)

3. She couldn't see any other way to attain her goal, so she changed her name from Miranda to James, and disguised herself as a man. (no)

4. It couldn't have been easy, but she kept the disguise up for her whole life. (hardly)

5. People who met her didn't guess her identity. (never)

6. She wasn't ever seen without her white lapdog, Psyche. (scarcely)

7. James Barry didn't hesitate to speak out against the conditions in leper colonies, prisons, and asylums she visited. (never)

8. These institutions weren't fit for human habitation. (barely)

9. In 1857, when James Barry was named inspector-general of Canada's military hospitals, there wasn't a higher medical post in the country. (no)

Dangling Modifiers

A dangling modifier is a modifying word or phrase that does not clearly indicate who or what is being described.

When it is not clear who or what a modifier is describing, the modifier is said to be **dangling.** Dangling modifiers can be words or phrases. Often, they can be quite funny. The comedian Groucho Marx used a dangling modifier in one of his jokes:

> "One morning I shot an elephant *in my pyjamas*. How he got in my pyjamas, I'll never know."
>
> (from the Marx Brothers movie, *Animal Crackers*)

To avoid dangling modifiers, try to keep modifiers as close as possible to the words they modify. In the following examples, the dangling modifiers are in italics, and the arrows point to the words they modify.

Dangling Adverb	I want to play the oboe *badly*.
Correct	I *badly* want to play the oboe.
Dangling Infinitive Phrase	*To graduate*, all of a student's assignments must be handed in.
Correct	*To graduate*, a student must hand in all of his or her assignments.
Dangling Prepositional Phrase	I saw a man pushing a baby carriage *through the window*.
Correct	*Through the window*, I saw a man pushing a baby carriage.
Dangling Participial Phrase	*Ringing loudly*, the boy was roused by the alarm clock.
Correct	*Ringing loudly*, the alarm clock roused the boy.

Phrases or participles at the beginning of a sentence often dangle. There are two reasons for this. First, because the person, thing, or action described by the phrase may not be close enough to the phrase. Remember that your readers will assume that the words immediately after the comma are the subject of the introductory phrase.

Unclear   Loudly barking, the man tried to calm the dog.
          (Why was the man barking?)

Clear   The man tried to calm the loudly barking dog.

The second possibility is that the subject of the introductory phrase is not stated at all in the rest of the sentence. In these cases, your reader can only figure out who or what the phrase refers to by reading your mind.

Unclear   Yawning sleepily, the sun rose.
          (The sun probably wasn't yawning, but who was?)

Clear   The sun rose as I was yawning sleepily.

Exercise 7   *Dangling Modifiers*

Rewrite the following sentences, eliminating any dangling modifiers. If a sentence is correct, make no changes.

1. To see the Rockies up close, good boots and a compass will take you further than a car.

2. Hiking along the trails, the mountains come alive.

3. I once saw a bear walking along the trail in my hiking boots!

4. To capture such moments, my camera stays close at hand.

5. This time, though, struggling with my lens cap, the huge beast lumbered off into the forest as I crouched in the bushes.

Exercise 8   *Modifier Usage Review*

Rewrite the following sentences using the correct word or words from those in parentheses. Correct any dangling modifiers.

1. Hardly (no, any) musical instrument is as well loved as the violin.

2. Played together, the violin sounds (beautiful, beautifully) with the piano.

3. The viola is slightly (larger, more large) than the violin.

4. Being smaller, the pitch is (higher, more high) than that of the viola.

5. Attracted by its high notes, the violin has been the favourite of some (real, really) famous composers, such as Mozart.

6. The double bass has the (deepest, most deeply) pitch of all the instruments in the string family.

7. The lute is the (ancientest, most ancient) ancestor of the guitar and the violin.

8. Many people in Elizabeth I's time played the lute (good, well).

9. Some people think the violin is the (more difficult, most difficult) instrument to play.

10. Both the stringed instruments and the piano sound (magnificent, magnificently) in an orchestra.

Using Verbs

A *verb* is a word that expresses an action or a state of being.

> A robot *welded* the parts together.
> Robots *are* perfect for dangerous jobs.

Classes of Verbs

Action verbs are verbs that tell what a subject does.

> Raffi *dived* into the water.
> Connie *danced* across the floor.

A *linking verb* connects the subject to a word that renames or describes the subject.

> Kim Campbell *was* Canada's first female prime minister.
> The moon *seems* huge tonight.
> Michael Ondaatje *is* a writer.
> The music *sounds* terrible.

All forms of the verb *to be* can be used as linking verbs. These forms include *am, is, are, was, were, be, been,* and *being.* Other verbs that are sometimes used as linking verbs are *appear, become, grow, look, seem, smell, sound, taste,* and *feel.*

If a verb can be replaced by a form of the verb *be* it is a linking verb. A verb that can't be replaced by a form of *be* is an action verb.

Lee *looked* good.
("Lee *was* good" makes sense, so *looked* is a linking verb.)

I *looked* at the squid.
("I *was* at the squid" doesn't sound right, so *looked* is an action verb.)

Helping verbs **help the action or linking verb.**

Helping verbs may be used with the main verb in a sentence to show the tense (time) or to indicate various shades of meaning.

I *may* **take** my pet gerbil to the vet.

helping verb   **main verb**

I *will* **take** guitar lessons next year.

helping verb   **main verb**

I *had been* **taking** lessons for a year before I made any progress.

helping verbs   **main verb**

Some common helping verbs are *can, could, will, would, shall, should, may, might*, and *must*. These verbs are always helping verbs. Even when they appear alone in a sentence, a main verb is always implied.

> *Will* you go to the party? I *may*.
> (The main verb *go* is implied in the answer:
> I may [go].)

Other common helping verbs include forms of *be, do*, and *have*.

Forms of *be*   am, is, are, was, were, be, been, being
Forms of *do*   do, does, did
Forms of *have*   have, has, had

Note that these three verbs are sometimes used as main verbs and sometimes as helping verbs.

> I **did** the test, but I *did*n't **know** all the answers.
> **main verb**   *helping verb*   **main verb**

Transitive and Intransitive Verbs

A verb is transitive if it needs a direct object to complete its meaning.

> Indira *addressed* the audience.
> Stanley *kissed* his lizard goodbye.

Do Behave

To remember which three verbs can be used as either helpers or main verbs, think of the expression "Do behave!" (do, be, have).

Reminder

A direct object tells who or what receives the action of the verb.

Intransitive verbs do not need a direct object to complete their meaning.

> The baby *cried*.
>
> Abel *swooned*.
>
> Jasmine *wilted*.
>
> They *rehearsed* every Thursday.

Exercise 1 *Types of Verbs*

Write the verbs in the following sentences. Identify each verb as action or linking. For each action verb, tell whether it is transitive or intransitive.

1. To the ancient Greeks, the earth was a beautiful goddess.

2. They called the earth *Ge*, the caretaker of all living things.

3. The name *Ge* is a part of the word *geology*, meaning "the study of the earth."

4. The Greeks also worshipped Demeter, another goddess.

5. This goddess protected the harvest and the fruits of the earth.

6. Hades, the selfish god of the underworld, adored Demeter's lovely daughter, Persephone.

7. Against Demeter's wishes, Hades took Persephone to the underworld.

8. Demeter grieved for her lost daughter, making the earth cold and bare.

9. Eventually, Persephone returned to her mother for part of each year.

10. According to the Greeks, the time when Persephone went with Demeter was spring, and the time when she descended to Hades was winter.

Prefixes and Suffixes

*A **prefix** is a group of letters added at the beginning of a word, to change its meaning. **Suffixes** are added to the end of a word. The suffix* phobia *means fear. What are these phobias?*

claustrophobia = fear of enclosed spaces

1. *agoraphobia*
2. *triskaidekaphobia*
3. *acrophobia*
4. *hydrophobia*
5. *arachnophobia*
6. *panophobia*
7. *monophobia*
8. *thanatophobia*

Answers

1. fear of open spaces 2. fear of the number 13 3. fear of heights 4. fear of water 5. fear of spiders 6. fear of everything 7. fear of being alone 8. fear of death

65

Verb Classes at a Glance

These two sentence charts offer a quick review of the different kinds of verbs.

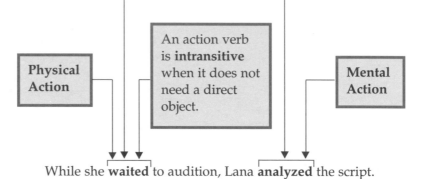

Action verbs tell what someone or something is doing. The action may be physical or mental.

An action verb is **transitive** when the action is directed from the subject (*Lana*) to the object of the verb (*script*). The object comes after the verb and tells who or what receives the action.

An action verb is **intransitive** when it does not need a direct object.

Physical Action

Mental Action

While she **waited** to audition, Lana **analyzed** the script.

Lana **may be** perfect for the lead role.

The Transitive Thief!

Some verbs can be transitive or intransitive, but with different meanings. In "The thief stole *my diamond tiara, then* stole *away," the first use of* stole *is transitive, and the second is intransitive.*

Helping verbs, or **auxiliary verbs**, help the action or linking verb. The most common helping verbs are forms of *be*: *am, is, are, was, were, be, been, being*; forms of *have*: *have, has, had*; forms of *do*: *do, does, did*; and *can, could, will, would, shall, should, may, might*, and *must*.

A **linking verb** shows a state of being. Instead of expressing action, it shows that something exists. Linking verbs are **intransitive** because they never take an object. A linking verb (*be*) links the subject (*Lana*) to a word in the predicate (*perfect*). In addition to the forms of *be*, the most common linking verbs are *look, smell, taste, feel, appear, sound, seem, become*, and *grow*.

Verb Usage

A sentence is not a sentence unless it has a verb. In fact, a verb is the only part of speech that can be a sentence on its own.

Stop!   Look!   Listen!

In most of your speaking and writing, you probably use verbs correctly without even thinking about it. In some cases, however, choosing the right verb might be confusing. This section will help you to avoid some common errors in verb usage.

The Principal Parts of Verbs

Every verb has four basic forms. These are known as the principal parts of a verb. The following are the principal parts of the verb *knit*.

Infinitive	Present Participle	Past	Past Participle
to knit	(is) knitting	knitted	(has) knitted

Regular Verbs

Most verbs form their principal parts in similar ways. The infinitive is the verb with *to* in front of it. To form the present participle, you add *-ing*. To form the past and past participles, you add *-ed*. Verbs that form their principal parts in these ways are called **regular verbs**. All regular verbs use the same form *(-ed)* for the past and past participle.

Principal Parts of Regular Verbs

Infinitive	Present Participle	Past	Past Participle
to rip	(is) ripping	ripped	(has) ripped
to check	(is) checking	checked	(has) checked
to climb	(is) climbing	climbed	(has) climbed
to dry	(is) drying	dried	(has) dried
to move	(is) moving	moved	(has) moved
to subtract	(is) subtracting	subtracted	(has) subtracted
to drop	(is) dropping	dropped	(has) dropped
to fry	(is) frying	fried	(has) fried
to howl	(is) howling	howled	(has) howled

Spelling

Note that a few regular verbs, such as rip *and* dry *change their spelling slightly when* -ing *or* -ed *is added.*

Quick Tip

When you use the infinitive form of a verb in a sentence, try not to put any words between the *to* and the verb. Dividing the *to* from the verb produces a split infinitive, which many people consider incorrect.

Split Infinitive: She tried to cautiously steer the canoe out of the rapids.
Correction: She tried cautiously to steer the canoe out of the rapids.

To Boldly Split...

Sometimes it just sounds better to split an infinitive. For example, can you imagine the following passage written any other way?

"These are the voyages of the starship Enterprise.

Its continuing mission: to explore strange new worlds,

To *seek out new life and new civilizations,*

To boldly go *where no one has gone before!"*

Irregular Verbs

Verbs that do not add *-ed* or *-d* to the infinitive to form the past and the past participle are **irregular verbs**.

Principal Parts of Some Commonly Used Irregular Verbs

Infinitive	Present Participle	Past	Past Participle
to be	(is) being	was, were	(has) been
to put	(is) putting	put	(has) put
to burst	(is) bursting	burst	(has) burst
to cost	(is) costing	cost	(has) cost
to set	(is) setting	set	(has) set
to sit	(is) sitting	sat	(has) sat
to bring	(is) bringing	brought	(has) brought
to lose	(is) losing	lost	(has) lost
to say	(is) saying	said	(has) said
to lay	(is) laying	laid	(has) laid
to lie	(is) lying	lay	(has) lain
to break	(is) breaking	broke	(has) broken
to choose	(is) choosing	chose	(has) chosen
to wear	(is) wearing	wore	(has) worn
to rise	(is) rising	rose	(has) risen
to begin	(is) beginning	began	(has) begun
to ring	(is) ringing	rang	(has) rung
to sing	(is) singing	sang	(has) sung
to come	(is) coming	came	(has) come
to do	(is) doing	done	(has) done
to go	(is) going	went	(has) gone

Because the principal parts of irregular verbs are formed in a variety of ways, you must either memorize these parts or refer to a dictionary. Most dictionaries list the principal parts of irregular verbs.

Infinitive   Past   Past Participle   Present Participle

Throw (thrō) *vt.* **threw, thrown, throw'ing** [ME *throwen*, to twist, wring, hurl OE *thrawan*, to throw, twist, akin to Ger *drehen*, to twist, turn IE base *ter-*, to rub with turning motion, bore THRASH, THREAD, Gr *teirein, terere*, to rub]

Exercise 2   *Principal Parts of Verbs in Dictionaries*

Make a chart with these headings: *Present, Present Participle, Past,* and *Past Participle.* List the principal parts from the following dictionary entries. Then, write a sentence using each principal part.

Example   **throw** (thrō) *vt.* **threw, thrown, throw'ing** [ME *throwen*, to twist, wring, hurl OE *thrawan*, to throw, twist, akin to Ger *drehen*, to twist, turn IE base *ter-*, to rub with turning motion, bore THRASH, THREAD, Gr *teirein, terere*, to rub] 1 to cause to fly through the air by releasing from the hand while the arm is in rapid motion; cast; hurl 2 to discharge through the air from a catapult, pump, gun, etc. 3 to hurl violently, as in anger, etc.; dash 4 to cause to fall; upset; overthrow; dislodge [*thrown* by a horse]

Answer

Present	Present Participle	Past	Past Participle
throw	throwing	threw	thrown

1. Please throw the ball.
2. The girls were throwing some practice pitches.
3. Ali threw the ball to the shortstop.
4. The pitcher had thrown a perfect game.

1. **freeze** (frēz) *vi.* **froze, fro'zen, freez'ing** < [ME *fresen* OE *freosan*, akin to OHG *friosan* (Ger *frieren*) < IE base *preus-*, to freeze, burn like cold > L *pruina*, hoarfrost, *pruna*, glowing coals] 1 to be formed into ice; be hardened or solidified by cold 2 to become clogged with ice 3 to be or become very cold

---

Past Participles

Since the past and the past participle of irregular verbs are sometimes different, how can you tell what the past participle of a verb will be? To find the past participle of any verb, ask yourself what form of the verb you would use after have. For example, the past of run is ran, but "I have ran" doesn't sound right. You would say "I have run," so the past participle of run is run.

2. **tear** (ter) *vt.* **tore, torn, tear'ing** [ME *teren* < OE *teren*, to rend, akin to Ger *zehren*, to destroy, consume < IE base **der-*, to skin, split > DRAB, DERMA] 1 to pull apart or separate into pieces by force; rip or rend (cloth, paper, etc.) 2 to make or cause by tearing or puncturing [to *tear* a hole in a dress] 3 to wound by tearing; lacerate [skin *torn* and bruised]

Progressive Forms

*Every verb tense can be written in a **progressive** form to show continuous action. To form the progressive, you add a form of the verb* be *to the verb's present participle.*

Normal Form

he sings
he sang
he will sing
he had sung
he has sung
he will have sung

Progressive Form

he is singing
he was singing
he will be singing
he had been singing
he has been singing
he will have been singing

Verb Tenses

Verbs are time-telling words. They not only tell of an action or a state of being, but they also tell *when* the action takes place. They tell whether the action or state of being is past, present, or future.

Verbs tell time in two ways:

1. changing their spelling
   walk → walked   sleep → slept

2. using helping verbs
   will creep   has crept   had crept

English verbs express six different times. Each verb has a form to express each of these six different times. The forms of a verb used to indicate time are called the **tenses** of a verb.

The Tenses of Verbs

Tense	Form	Use
Present	Add *-s* or *-es* for third person singular.	To show an action that happens now: *Let's leave.* To tell about something that happens regularly: *The geyser erupts every ninety minutes.* To tell about constant action: *The earth revolves around the sun.*
Past	Add *-d* or *-ed* to the present. If the verb is irregular, use the past form.	To show an action that was completed in the past: The *Druids built Stonehenge.*
Future	Use *will* or *shall* with the present form.	To show an action that will occur in the future: *Our baseball team will win the championship next year.*
Present Perfect	Use *has* or *have* with the past participle.	To show an action that began in the past and continues into the present: *The pyramids have stood for thousands of years.*
Past Perfect	Use *had* with the past participle.	To show an action in the past that came before another action in the past: *We had seen lightning shortly before the fire began.*
Future Perfect	Use *will have* or *shall have* with the past participle.	To show an action in the future that will happen before another future action or time: *The concert will have ended by the time you are ready.*

Exercise 3   *Verb Tenses*

Write each sentence in your notebook, filling in the blank or blanks with the correct form of the verb described in parentheses.

Example   Today's students of writing _____ tomorrow's movies and television programs. (future of *to create*)

Answer   Today's students of writing will create tomorrow's movies and television programs.

1. The director _____ to start shooting next week's episode yesterday. (past perfect of *to hope*)

2. However, the script for the episode _____ terrible. (past of *to be*)

3. This terrible script _____ filming and is costing a lot of money. (present perfect of *to delay*)

4. What _____ the director _____? (future of *to do*)

5. She will do what she _____ in the past. (present perfect of *to do*)

6. She _____ in her story editors. (future of *to call*)

7. A story editor is a professional screenplay editor who _____ on the staff of a television program. (present of *to work*)

8. By the time the director is ready to start shooting the episode tomorrow morning, the story editors _____ the screenplay several times. (future perfect of *to rewrite*)

9. There is no professional story editor who _____ not _____ many such rushed revisions. (present perfect of *to complete*)

10. Screenwriters and story editors _____ under a great deal of pressure because of the demands from producers, directors, actors, marketing people, network executives, and just about everyone else! (present of *to be*)

Shake Up Your Verbs!

Don't weaken strong verbs by smothering them in unnecessary phrases. Here are some examples of smothered verbs.

Smothered	Uncovered
to be in agreement	to agree
to take action	to act

Smothered verbs have almost no impact. *Avoid them wherever possible!*

Can you uncover the smothered verbs in the following phrases?

1. to be in attendance
2. to make an attempt
3. to pay a compliment
4. to take into consideration
5. to arrive at a conclusion
6. to have a need
7. to give a description
8. to resemble in nature
9. to give encouragement
10. to extend an invitation

Verbs with Verve

This quotation from American writer F. Scott Fitzgerald makes good use of the power of verbs.

"Mostly, we authors must repeat ourselves—that's the truth. We have two or three great moving experiences in our lives—experiences so great and moving that it doesn't seem at the time that anyone else has been caught up and pounded and dazzled and astonished and beaten and broken and rescued and illuminated and rewarded and humbled in just that way ever before."

Answers

*1. to attend 2. to attempt 3. to compliment 4. to consider 5. to conclude
6. to need 7. to describe 8. to resemble 9. to encourage 10. to invite*

Active and Passive Voice

The tense of a verb indicates the time of the action. The *voice* of the verb tells us about the role of the subject in the sentence.

If the subject of a verb is the actor in the sentence, the verb is in the *active voice.*

> She delivered the paper.
>
> Dominic bounced the ball.
>
> The government passed the bill.

The active voice is the voice that you use most often in both spoken and written English.

If the subject of the verb is acted upon, the verb is in the *passive voice.*

Transitive verbs are those that need a direct object to complete their meaning. Intransitive verbs do not need a direct object.

Only transitive verbs can be written in the passive voice.

> The jockey was thrown from the saddle.
> The fire was extinguished by the firefighters.
> My wallet has been stolen.

The passive voice is useful if you do not know who did the action, if the actor is obvious or unimportant, or if you want to emphasize who received the action rather than who performed it. In other cases, it is usually better to use the active voice, because it is simpler and more direct.

Whodunnit?

Often, the actor is not named in a passive voice sentence, either because it is not known, or because it is deemed unimportant. Sometimes, you can guess who the actor is, as in "The jockey was thrown from the saddle." You probably assume that the actor here is a horse.

To change a sentence in the passive voice to the active voice, make the actor the subject of the sentence.

Passive The guests were greeted by the host.
Active The host greeted the guests.

Passive The Riddler was foiled by Batman.
Active Batman foiled the Riddler.

Passive I was woken by the scream of a train whistle.
Active The scream of a train whistle woke me.

Quick Tip

The actor in a passive voice sentence is often named in a prepositional phrase beginning with *by*.

> The room was cleaned by the janitor.
> (The janitor is the person who cleaned.)

> Hossam was hit by the ball.
> (The ball is the thing that hit.)

Exercise 4 *Changing Passive Voice to Active Voice*

Rewrite each of the following sentences, changing passive voice to active. If a sentence is already in the active voice, write "correct."

1. Computer networks can be accessed by anyone with a home computer and a modem.

2. These networks can be used by subscribers to get information about everything from stock market reports to video selections.

3. Discussion groups, called newsgroups, can be joined by people with similar interests.

4. Using a network to "talk" to others can be fun.

5. The interesting thing about newsgroups is that your age, sex, and race can't be seen by other users in the group.

6. As one user put it, "You can be anyone you want."

7. Computer networks have serious uses as well; television and radio were shut down by coup leaders during the 1991 attempt to overthrow Mikhail Gorbachev.

8. The Internet was used by Boris Yeltsin to get information and to maintain contact with the West.

9. Some people worry that face-to-face human interaction will be reduced by networks.

10. Also, the huge amount of information available through these "information superhighways" might be abused by governments.

Emoticons

Body language doesn't come through on a computer screen. To replace the clues we get from seeing each other face-to-face, computer users sometimes end their newsgroup messages with emoticons, or smileys. Here are some common emoticons. (To read them, tilt your head to the left!)

:-)	*smiley face*
:-(	*sad face*
;-)	*wink*
8-0	*complete surprise*
:-c	*very unhappy*
:-,	*smirking face*
I-(	*stayed up too late*
8-)	*person wearing glasses*
?-(	*person with black eye*
8-]	*state of bliss*

Cyberspace Abbreviations

Here are some of the shorthand expressions used by newsgroup users to shorten the amount of typing they have to do.

AAMOF	as a matter of fact	**OTOH**	on the other hand
AFAIK	as far as I know	**ROFL**	rolling on the floor laughing
BFHD	big fat hairy deal	**TANSTAAFL**	there ain't no such thing as a free lunch
BTW	by the way		
FWIW	for what it's worth	**TTYL**	talk to you later
IMHO	in my humble opinion	**WYSIWYG**	what you see is what you get
IOW	in other words		

Commonly Confused Verbs

Some verbs are confusing because, while having different meanings, they are similar in form. Three of these confusing verb pairs are *lie* and *lay*, *rise* and *raise*, and *sit* and *set*.

Lie	to lie	lying	lay	lain
Lay	to lay	laying	laid	laid

Lie means "to rest in a flat position," "to be in a certain place," or "to exist." *Lie* never has a direct object.
Lay means "to place." It almost always has a direct object.

Before I lie on the beach, I lay down my towel.

Raise	raise	raising	raised	raised
Rise	rise	rising	rose	risen

Raise means "to lift" or "to make something go up." It almost always has a direct object.
Rise means "to go upward." *Rise* never has a direct object.

When they *raised* the sunken tanker, more crude oil *rose* to the surface.

Sit	sit	sitting	sat	sat
Set	set	setting	set	set

Sit means "to occupy a seat." *Sit* never has a direct object.
Set means "to place." *Set* almost always has a direct object.

I will *sit* at my desk and *set* down my thoughts.

Other Confusing Words

You will find a list of other commonly confused words beginning on page 133.

Quick Tip

Lie, *rise*, and *sit* are all intransitive, meaning they never take a direct object. Since all three words contain the letter *i*, it is easy to remember that they are **i**ntransitive.

Exercise 5   *Confusing Verbs*

Write the correct verb form of the two verbs given in parentheses.

1. There used to be over fifty indigenous languages spoken in Canada; some of these have already died out, and the number on the endangered list is (rising, raising).

2. Many linguists are (rising, raising) the alarm, claiming that few Native languages are safe from extinction.

3. But Native groups are not taking the threat to their languages (lying, laying) down.

4. Part of the answer (lies, lays) with computers, which can be used to store information, and to make it easier for Native speakers to communicate in their own languages.

5. For example, hope for the survival of one Native language— Halq'emeylem, spoken by the Sto:lo has now been (raised, risen), thanks to a computerized dictionary.

6. A linguist (sat, set) down with Sto:lo Elders and taught them to write down their language—which has no traditional written form—using the Roman alphabet; they, in turn, taught him words, which he added to his dictionary.

7. At a recent conference, the possibility of devising a keyboard for use by speakers of Inuktitut and Cree was (risen, raised) by some Native groups.

8. These two linguistic groups both use syllabic symbols, based on Pittman shorthand, to (set, sit) down their languages.

9. Since the language groups that use the syllabic system are very different, a new keyboard will have to be (laid, lain) out so that both groups can use it easily.

Syllabics

The syllabic system used by some Native groups was developed by English missionaries. Each symbol stands for a syllable, rather than just a letter. Here are some examples.

△ i	▷ u	◁ a
∧ pi	＞ pu	＜ pa
∩ ti	⊃ tu	⊂ ta
P ki	d ku	b ka
ſ gi	J gu	L ga

New Words in Inuktitut

English	Inuktitut	Literal Translation
computer	qaritaujaq	like a brain
satellite	qangatatitausimajuq	an item raised to the heavens
fax	sukatunik titraut	fast letters
ozone layer	sikajuap igalavja	covering over the earth

Exercise 6   *Verb Usage Review*

Rewrite the following sentences, inserting the correct verb forms. Change the underlined clauses from the passive voice to the active voice.

1. In January of 1994, <u>Los Angeles was shaken by an earthquake, in which many residents were killed and extensive damage was caused to buildings and highways</u>.

2. Despite the devastation <u>that was brought by the early-morning quake</u>, you could say it (past perfect of *to choose*) a good time to happen.

3. The day of the quake was a holiday, so traffic was light; the death toll would have (*risen, raised*) dramatically if the tremors (past perfect of *to happen*) on a regular working day.

4. Los Angeles (*sits, sets*) on the San Andreas fault, where two of the earth's plates meet.

5. The epicentre of the quake (*lie, lay*) in the San Fernando Valley, near Northridge.

6. Anyone who figures out a way to pinpoint where and when the next earthquake will hit (future perfect of *to make*) an important discovery.

7. Some Chinese studies (present perfect of *to show*) that animals (future of *to run*) from their lairs in the hours before a quake hits.

8. Snakes that live underground will (*rise, raise*) to the surface, even if the weather is cold enough to kill them.

9. In Los Angeles, <u>many dogs and cats were lost by residents</u> just days before the quake (past of *to hit*).

10. <u>It is believed by some scientists</u> that animals (present of *to know*) when a quake (future of *to occur*) because they sense the changes in the earth's magnetic field.

Subject-Verb Agreement

A verb must agree in number with its subject.

When the subject of a sentence is singular, its verb must also be singular. When the subject is plural, its verb must also be plural. This is called **subject-verb agreement.**

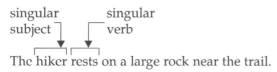

The hiker rests on a large rock near the trail.

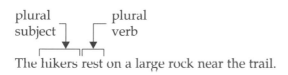

The hikers rest on a large rock near the trail.

Most of the time, the singular and plural forms of verbs will not cause problems for you.

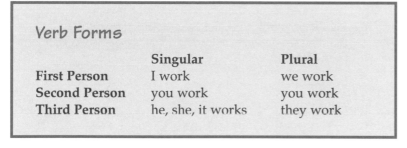

Verb Forms

	Singular	Plural
First Person	I work	we work
Second Person	you work	you work
Third Person	he, she, it works	they work

However, the verb *to be* does not follow the usual pattern. In the chart on the next page, notice that *to be* has special forms in both the present and the past tenses in all three persons.

> **Reminder**
>
> *When a word refers to one thing, it is **singular**. When it refers to more than one thing, it is **plural**. The **number** of a word refers to whether the word is singular or plural.*

Forms of *To Be*				
	Present Tense		**Past Tense**	
	Singular	**Plural**	**Singular**	**Plural**
First Person	I am	we are	I was	we were
Second Person	you are	you are	you were	you were
Third Person	he, she, it is	they are	he, she, it was	they were

The most common errors involving forms of the verb *to be* are using the words *you, we,* and *they* with the singular verb *was*. Remember to avoid saying or writing *you was, we was,* and *they was.*

Phrases Between a Subject and a Verb

Do not be fooled by other nouns in a sentence. Be sure that the verb agrees with its subject.

You are more likely to have a problem with subject-verb agreement if you cannot identify the subject in a sentence. To find the subject, first find the verb and then ask *who* or *what* before it.

The *flower* with bright red petals *is* a geranium.
(Since *is* is the verb, ask *what is*? *Flower*, not *petals*, is the subject.)

In the preceding sentence, "with bright red petals" is a **prepositional phrase**. Be especially careful when a prepositional phrase falls between the subject and the verb. Do not be fooled by the noun that appears in the phrase. Make the verb agree in number with the subject.

The *books* on the shelf *are* all mysteries.
(The subject is *books*, not *shelf*.)

Prepositions

Commonly used prepositions include the following: about, above, across, after, as, at, before, between, by, during, for, from, in, inside, into, like, near, of, off, on, over, since, through, to, until, up, upon, with, without.

uick Tip

To decide which word is the subject, say the sentence without the phrase. If you have chosen the correct word as the subject, the sentence will make sense without the phrase.

Exercise 1   *Sentences with Phrases*

Choose the verb that agrees with the subject.

1. Tests of any kind (scare, scares) many people.

2. Students in high school (fear, fears) tests and exams more than they fear dental visits!

3. Characteristics of test anxiety (include, includes) headaches, sweaty palms, and feelings of panic.

4. To relieve anxiety, students of all ages (need, needs) to learn to relax.

5. Relaxation classes after school (help, helps) students learn how to deal with stress.

6. The teachers in this type of class (explain, explains) relaxation techniques.

7. Fearful students in this class (learn, learns) how to replace negative thoughts with positive ones.

8. A class about study skills also (helps, help) reduce test anxiety.

9. Classes like this (give, gives) students more confidence.

10. Successful results on a test (is, are) sometimes the best way to relieve test anxiety!

Indefinite Pronouns as Subjects

Use a singular verb with a singular indefinite pronoun, and use a plural verb with a plural indefinite pronoun.

uick Tip

One way to remember which indefinite pronouns are singular is to look at the word endings that refer to one thing: *-other, -one, -body, -thing*. Also, many of the singular pronouns are compound—for example, *anything, someone*; none of the plural pronouns is compound.

Indefinite pronouns do not refer to a definite person or thing. Some indefinite pronouns are singular, some are plural, and some can be either. For the definite pronouns that are always singular or plural, the correct verb choice will often be the one that sounds right to you.

Incorrect Everyone have a project to complete.
Correct Everyone has a project to complete.
(*Everyone* is singular; it takes a singular verb, *has*.)

Incorrect Both of the movies is in French.
Correct Both of the movies are in French.
(*Both* is plural; it takes a plural verb, *are*.)

The indefinite pronouns that are either singular or plural cause the most difficulties in subject-verb agreement. If the pronoun refers to one thing, it is singular and requires a singular verb. If the pronoun refers to several things or to things that can be counted, it is plural and requires a plural verb.

Singular All of the food was eaten.
(*All* refers to a single quantity of food, so it requires the singular verb *was*.)

Plural All of the dishes were washed.
(*All* refers to several dishes, so it requires the plural verb *were*.)

Indefinite Pronouns

Singular indefinite pronouns include either, neither, anybody, everyone, something, each, much, one.

Plural indefinite pronouns are both, few, many, several.

Those that can be singular or plural include all, enough, most, plenty, any, more, none, some.

Remember that *none* can be plural. It is plural if it refers to more than one person, place, or thing. It is singular if it refers to only one person, place, or thing.

Singular None of the street is visible from here.
Plural None of the streets are visible from here.

Exercise 2   *Agreement with Indefinite Pronouns*

Choose the correct verb forms from those in parentheses.

1.   Everyone (wear, wears) clothes, and all of us (make, makes) some kind of fashion statement every day.

2.   Most of us (thinks, think) that people wear clothes for warmth and modesty, but even the earliest hunter-gatherers in tropical climates wore animal skins.

3. Clearly, one of the reasons for wearing clothes (are, is) the status they give us.

4. Some of the clothing styles worn by women and men throughout the ages (look, looks) awfully strange.

5. Both of the sexes (has, have) worn uncomfortable, and even dangerous fashions, just to look like everybody else.

6. For example, in the fifteenth century, men wore soft leather shoes with long pointed toes that had to be held up with chains so the wearer wouldn't trip over them; nowadays, everybody (is, are) a lot happier in running shoes!

7. Few women (think, thinks) that waist-cinching and corsets are due for a comeback in the 1990s.

8. All of us (is, are) "victims of fashion" in some sense, though; what would your friends say if you showed up for school in your pyjamas or in a hoop skirt?

Palindromes

Palindromes (pronounced PAL-in-dromes) are words, phrases, sentences, or even numbers that read the same backwards and forwards.

Palindromic Words:
radar, kayak, level, rotor

Palindromic Sentences:
Madam, I'm Adam.
Rats live on no evil star.
Sit on Otis.
Able was I ere I saw Elba.
Was it Eliot's toilet I saw?
Doc, note, I dissent: a fast never
prevents a fatness; I diet on cod!

Here is another kind of palindrome. The words, not the letters, read the same backwards and forwards:

Bores are people that say that people are bores.
Does milk machinery milk does?
So patient a doctor to doctor a patient so.
You can cage a swallow, can't you, but you can't swallow a cage, can you?

Write the subject of each of the following sentences.
Then write the verb that agrees in number with the subject.

1.   Many great artists (was, were) living and working in Italy in the fifteenth century.

2.   The paintings from this period in history (hang, hangs) on museum walls all over the world.

3.   Everyone in my art class (recognizes, recognize) the name of Leonardo da Vinci.

4.   Most of da Vinci's artistic achievements (reflects, reflect) the brilliance of his curious mind.

5.   Few of my classmates (know, knows) that da Vinci was the leading scientist of his age.

6.   Most art students (know, knows) that da Vinci sought to understand the inner workings of everything he painted.

7.   Because Leonardo da Vinci worked on so many kinds of projects simultaneously, many of his projects (were, was) never completed.

8.   One of his artistic achievements (are, is) called *chiaroscuro*, meaning "clear-dark" in Italian.

9.   This artistic technique, involving the use of light and background shadow, (makes, make) people seem realistic.

10. Everyone in the art world (understands, understand) the value of da Vinci's legacy.

Compound Subjects

Use a plural verb with most compound subjects joined by *and*. Use a verb that agrees with the subject nearer the verb when the words in a compound subject are joined by *or* or *nor*.

A compound subject is two or more subjects used with the same verb. Most compound subjects that contain the word *and* are plural and take a plural verb.

> Track and swimming are my best sports.
> Speed and endurance help an athlete to excel.

When the parts of a compound subject are connected by the conjunction *or* or *nor,* you need to look at the subject that is closer to the verb to decide if the verb should be singular or plural.

> Neither Su-Yin nor her *friends* work after school.
> Either the cyclists or the *gymnast* appears next.

Sentences with one singular and one plural subject usually sound better if you place the plural subject last, so the verb is plural.

> Either the gymnast or the cyclists appear next.

Reminder

If a compound subject is preceded by each *or* every, *use a singular verb.*

Each *dog and owner* receives *a prize.*

Every *girl and boy* deserves *the same opportunity.*

Exercise 4 *Compound Subjects*

Write the form of the verb that agrees with the subject.

1. Liz and Vivek (loves, love) to read mysteries.

2. Neither Liz nor her friend (understand, understands) how difficult it is to write a mystery novel.

3. Liz and he (decides, decide) to write a mystery.

4. Most people don't realize that neither the characters nor the plot (is, are) easily created.

5. Amateur sleuths or a private detective (is, are) essential in any good mystery.

6. Liz and Vivek (develops, develop) a plot that revolves around a grisly murder, of course!

7. A victim and many suspects (appears, appear) in different chapters of their story.

8. Both obvious clues and red herrings always (seems, seem) to lead the reader to a solution.

9. Strong dialogue and interesting plot developments (help, helps) to build suspense and keep the reader wondering what will happen next.

10. Neither the authors nor their classmates (know, knows) yet how the mystery will be solved!

Agreement in Inverted Sentences

In most sentences the subject comes before the verb. However, sometimes the subject and the verb are inverted.

Regular Order The growl of a tiger came from the jungle.
(The subject *growl* comes before the verb *came*.)

Inverted Order From the jungle came the growl of a tiger.
(The subject *growl* comes after the verb *came*.)

Subjects and verbs are often inverted in questions.

> Is deep space really cold?
> (The subject is *space*. The verb is *Is*.)

> Are the aurora borealis and the northern lights
> the same thing?
> (The compound subject is *the aurora borealis* and *the northern lights*. The verb is *Are*.)

Subjects and verbs are also sometimes inverted after the words *there, where*, or *here*.

> Here is a mummy from ancient Ecuador.
> (The subject is *mummy*. The verb is *is*.)

> Where are your mittens?
> (The subject is *mittens*. The verb is *are*.)

A verb must always agree with its subject, even if the subject and the verb are inverted.

Incorrect In the sky was many strange, multicoloured lights.

Correct In the sky were many strange, multicoloured lights.

Exercise 5   *Agreement in Inverted Sentences*

Rewrite the following paragraph, choosing the correct form of each verb in parentheses.

1. Across the sky (shoot, shoots) a tiny speck of light.

2. There, on the horizon, (is, are) the place where the light seems to land.

3. (Was, Were) it simply a trick of the light or of the imagination, or (was, were) it something real?

4. In the sky (is, are) many strange lights.

5. (Is, Are) some of them flying saucers?

6. Where there (is, are) flying saucers, there (is, are) usually overactive imaginations.

7. There (is, are) often more rational explanations.

8. In the sky at night (appear, appears) many things—such as meteors, satellites, balloons, and weather phenomena—that (look, looks) like flying saucers but (isn't, aren't).

9. (Is, Are) reports of flying saucers always fanciful?

10. There (is, are) no one who really knows.

Agreement Problems with *Doesn't* and *Don't*

Use *doesn't* with singular subjects and with the personal pronouns *he, she,* and *it.* Use *don't* with plural subjects and with the personal pronouns *I, we, you,* and *they.*

For many writers, the words *doesn't* and *don't* create agreement problems. Keep in mind that these words are contractions for *does not* and *do not.*

Incorrect   *Doesn't* the stars seem brilliant tonight?

Correct   *Don't* the stars seem brilliant tonight?

Incorrect   *Don't* the moon seem eerie tonight?

Correct   *Doesn't* the moon seem eerie tonight?

Exercise 6   Doesn't and Don't

Choose the form of the verb that agrees in number with the subject.

1. Since the members of my family (doesn't, don't) agree about music, the room where we keep our CD player has become a battlefield.

2. Other people (doesn't, don't) understand the problem until they live in this household for at least a week.

3. My grandparents (doesn't, don't) like loud music at all.

4. My mother and my older sister (doesn't, don't) like country music.

5. It (doesn't, don't) matter to me—I listen to country music whenever I'm in the mood.

6. My older brother (doesn't, don't) like classical music, but my younger sister turns up Beethoven full blast whenever she can.

7. My younger brother (doesn't, don't) listen to anything I say, but he has listened to the same sing-along-with-Mr. Rogers tape at least a thousand times.

8. My brother and I (doesn't, don't) understand why anyone would like opera, but my father sings along with *Madame Butterfly*.

9. My family and I (doesn't, don't) agree about any music except elevator music: we all hate it!

10. Our neighbours (doesn't, don't) enjoy our varied musical tastes; they'd prefer the sound of silence instead.

Hopeless Headlines

Headline writers have the difficult job of communicating information in a small amount of space. Not only do they have to choose their words carefully, but they have to order them correctly! Here are some headlines that didn't quite work.

- BOY, 14, BEATS WOMAN WITH PRIZE SPONGE CAKE

- TOWN TO DROP SCHOOL BUS WHEN OVER-PASS IS READY

- CARIBBEAN ISLANDS DRIFT TO LEFT

- TWO CONVICTS EVADE NOOSE; JURY HUNG

- MINERS REFUSE TO WORK AFTER DEATH

- LAWYERS GIVE POOR FREE LEGAL ADVICE

- SQUAD HELPS DOG BITE VICTIM

- DOCTOR TESTIFIES IN HORSE SUIT

Sentence Combining

A sentence is a group of words that expresses a complete thought. A sentence may be simple, compound, or complex.

Simple Sentences

A simple sentence contains only one subject and one predicate.

Throughout this book you have been studying sentences. You know that a sentence has two basic parts, the *subject* and the *predicate*.

Subject	Predicate
Fred	dithered.
The dog	sniffed the rose.
The camper in the tent	studied the map of the area.

Simple sentences such as these are useful because they are a direct and forceful way of telling your reader something. However, if every sentence you wrote was like these, your writing would sound choppy and disjointed. Fortunately, there are several ways to combine sentences and parts of sentences to make your writing more interesting.

Combining Sentence Parts

You can combine two simple sentences that have an element in common by using a coordinating conjunction (*and, or, nor, for, but, so,* or *yet*). Some of the parts that can be combined are subjects, verbs, and objects. We call sentence parts that are joined like this **compounds.** In the examples below, notice how the words in italics disappear in the combined version.

Compound Subject   Harry *was jittery.* +
Grace was jittery. =
Harry **and** Grace **were** jittery.

Compound Verb   The dolphins swam. +
The dolphins jumped. =
The dolphins swam **and** jumped.

Compound Predicate   Sunil ran for the bus. +
He couldn't catch it. =
Sunil ran for the bus **but** couldn't catch it.

Compound Object   Ajai carried the cheese. +
He also carried the bread. =
Ajai carried the cheese **and** the bread.

The coordinating conjunctions are *and, or, nor, for, but, so,* and *yet.* Think of them as the parts of a Russian-sounding name: Andor Norfor Butsoyet.

Any part of a simple sentence can be compound. That is, it may contain more than one part connected by a conjunction, such as *and,* or *or.*

Remember that when you combine parts of a simple sentence, the result is still a simple sentence.

Powerful Paragraphs on Cue

Remember: **CUE = C**oherence **U**nity **E**mphasis

COHERENCE

- State your ideas simply and straightforwardly.

- Arrange your ideas according to one of the following frameworks:

    - order of time (chronological)
    - order of space or position (topical)
    - order of importance (climactic)
    - order of sense (logical)

- Use connecting words and phrases to show how your ideas are related, and to make your essay flow smoothly from idea to idea.

- Write from one point of view.

UNITY

- Begin each paragraph with a topic sentence.

- Make sure every sentence in the paragraph is closely related to the topic sentence.

- Never waver. Let your readers know how you want them to feel, think, or act.

EMPHASIS

- Start with an arresting sentence.

- Finish with a memorable idea.

- Every so often, surprise your reader.

- Use the most interesting words you can find.

- Use imagery and figures of speech that will grab your reader's attention.

Linking Words

Some common linking words and phrases: therefore, although, since, in spite of this, in addition, similarly, afterwards, firstly, it follows that.

Unity

United the paragraph stands,
Divided it crumbles apart;
One subject it firmly demands,
And a good topic sentence to start.

Ideas to add oomph! to your paragraphs

quotations	repetition	specific names and places
anecdotes	illustrations	ugly-sounding words (cacophony)
contrast	humour	pleasant-sounding words
facts	irony	(euphony)

Combining Sentences

Create a compound sentence by joining two or more simple sentences together.

A simple sentence, with or without compound elements, contains one principal clause. When you join together two or more simple sentences, the result is a **compound sentence** with two principal clauses.

Simple Sentences	The Shepherds adopted a little girl. They named her Claudine.
Compound Sentence	The Shepherds adopted a little girl, and they named her Claudine.

Simple sentences can be joined in one of three ways.

1. You can join simple sentences by using a comma and a coordinating conjunction.

Simple Sentences	The car overheated. We made it to Lake Louise anyway.
Compound Sentence	The car overheated, **but** we made it to Lake Louise anyway.
Simple Sentence	Mary Ann Shadd spoke out against prejudice and started a newspaper.
Compound Sentence	Mary Ann Shadd spoke out against prejudice and **she** started a newspaper.

2. You can also join simple sentences by using a semicolon.

Compound Sentence	The car overheated; we made it to Lake Louise anyway.

3. Finally, you can join simple sentences by using a semicolon, a conjunctive adverb such as *however* or *therefore,* and a comma.

Compound Sentence	The car overheated; **however,** we made it to Lake Louise anyway.

Two simple sentences should be joined together only if they are related in meaning. Do not join sentences that are unrelated.

Incorrect   Canada is a leader in the field of telecommunications, and I have been studying sentence combining.

Exercise 1   *Simple and Compound Sentences*

Combine each pair of sentences into one sentence, and indicate whether you have created a simple sentence or a compound sentence.

1. Woolly mammoths lived over ten thousand years ago. They lived in North America, Europe, and Asia.

2. Long tusks were characteristic of the mammoths. Enormous size was also characteristic of the mammoths.

3. Modern elephants stand about three metres high at the shoulder. Mammoths stood about four metres high.

4. Years ago, scientists in Siberia discovered a peculiar mammoth. They also excavated it.

5. The mammoth was frozen. It had buttercups in its mouth.

6. Thousands of years ago, something had frozen the mammoth. This force had also frozen the plants.

7. The fresh green plants mean that the weather must have been warm. The freezing mammoth required a sudden, fierce cold.

8. For years now, scientists have speculated about what might have caused the sudden deep freeze of the Siberian mammoth. Crackpots have also speculated about what caused this deep freeze.

9. To this day, no one has solved this mystery. No one has a clue as to how to go about solving it.

10. Somehow that mammoth was warm one moment and frozen solid the next moment! Those buttercups were also warm one moment and frozen solid the next moment!

Simple Sentence or Principal Clause?

A principal clause is a group of words that contains a subject and a verb, and which makes sense on its own. A simple sentence is the same thing as a principal clause. We call it a principal clause when it is used in a compound or a complex sentence, and a simple sentence when it is used on its own, with proper punctuation.

Portmanteau Words

Portmanteau words are two words packaged as one. For example, *smog* is a combination of *smoke* and *fog*. Identify the words that have emerged from the following pairs.

1.   breakfast + lunch

2.   war + orphan

3.   French + English

4.   splash + spatter

5.   elevator + escalate

6.   motor + cavalcade

7.   chirp + tweet

8.   blow + spurt

9.   happen + circumstance

10.   mist + drizzle

Answers
*1. brunch 2. warphan 3. Frenglish 4. splatter 5. escalator 6. motorcade
7. cheep 8. blurt 9. happenstance 10. mizzle*

Complex Sentences

A sentence that is made up of one or more subordinate clauses and a principal clause is called a *complex sentence.*

A **complex sentence** is what you get when you add a subordinate clause to a simple sentence. You can join two simple sentences to make a complex sentence if one expresses a main idea or action, while the other tells something about the circumstances or the timing of the main idea or action.

You can't go out. You have to do the dishes first.

You can't go out **until** you have done the dishes.

principal clause   subordinate clause

A subordinate clause may be introduced by a pronoun such as *who, whoever, whom, whomever, whose, what, whatever, that,* or *which.* It may also be introduced by a subordinating conjunction.

Synonyms

How many synonyms (words with similar meaning) for join *can you think of? For example...*

Repairs *bind, glue, stitch, weld, solder...*

Technology *rivet, splice, velcro, yoke...*

Medicine *graft, suture, fuse...*

Economics *merge, amalgamate...*

Politics *ally, equate, confederate, league...*

Social Life *couple, marry, associate, embrace...*

Other *attach, connect, link, bridge, meet...*

Now try making a list of antonyms (words with opposite meaning) for join.

Subordinating Conjunctions

Time	after, as, as long as, as soon as, before, since, until, when, whenever, while
Manner	as, as if
Place	where, wherever
Cause or Reason	because, since
Comparison	as, as much as, than
Condition	although, as long as, even if, even though, if, provided that, though, unless, while
Purpose	in order that, so that, that

To make a subordinate clause into a sentence, you have to add a principal clause (a simple sentence) to it.

> We must wait (principal clause) +
> until the package is sent (subordinate clause) =
> We must wait until the package is sent.
> (complex sentence)

Exercise 2   *Complex Sentences*

Write down the following complex sentences. Underline each principal clause once and each subordinate clause twice.

Example   This is the book that I told you about.
Answer   <u>This is the book</u> <u><u>that I told you about.</u></u>

1. This is a picture of a dog who meant a lot to me.

2. The name that we gave him was Norman.

3. Norman believed he was human.

4. Although he was just a small brown mongrel, he thought he was very fierce.

5. When we walked through the field with the cows in it, Norman would stand still and bark loudly.

6. However, if a cow started to move toward him, he would start whimpering and run between our legs!

7. Another time, at the lake, he barked indignantly at a piece of grass floating in the water whenever anyone was close enough to hear.

8. When someone finally fished it out and laid it on the shore, he grabbed it and shook it until it was well and truly dead!

9. On summer nights, his favourite place to sleep was in the barn, where it was cool.

10. In winter, he spent his evenings on my bed, because he liked to make a nest out of my quilt.

Exercise 3 *Compound and Complex Sentences*

Create one compound and one complex sentence from each of the following principal clauses.

Example   no one was injured by the tremor

Answer   No one was injured by the tremor, but it left a lasting impression. (compound sentence)
No one was injured by the tremor, although many people were scared by it. (complex sentence)

1. the lights went out

2. the party died down

3. it rained on Saturday

4. the train was pulling out of the station

5. the dog was not properly trained

6. the fire was out

7. that man wrote the story

8. I was overwhelmed by emotion

9. it was very foggy

10. the movie is almost over

Exercise 4 *Review and Application*

Choose two of the following topics and write a brief
paragraph (five or six sentences) on each. Vary the types of sentences you use. Label each sentence as simple, compound, or
complex.

Music	Television
Cars	Food
UFOs	Applesauce
Sports	Toenails

Capitalization

One of the purposes of capitalization is to call attention to particularly important words. Of course, you use capitalization at the beginning of sentences and for names. However, there are some other capitalization rules that writers need to know in order to distinguish certain words or groups of words. Most words that are capitalized fall into one of two broad categories: proper nouns and proper adjectives; and first words in groups of words. Listed below are some more specific rules and examples of capitalization. You can use this section as a reference when you are in doubt about whether to capitalize a word.

Rules of Capitalization

Capitalize proper nouns and adjectives.

A **proper noun** is the name of a specific person, place, thing, or idea. Proper nouns are capitalized and common nouns are not. A **proper adjective** is an adjective formed from a proper noun; it is also capitalized.

Common Noun	mountains
Proper Noun	Andes
Proper Adjective	Andean

Capitalize people's names and initials that stand for names.

W. O. Mitchell   Alannah Myles

Capitalize titles and abbreviations of titles when used before people's names or in direct address.

Professor Susan Hill   Dr. R. Shah

Capitalize a title used without a person's name if it refers to a head of state or a person in another important position.

> the Prime Minister of Canada
> the Queen of England

Always capitalize the pronoun *I*.

> Anthony and I cooked the curried vegetables.

Capitalize words indicating family relationships when the words are used as names or parts of names.

> Dad and Nana are looking forward to the arrival of Uncle Hal.

If the word is preceded by an article or a possessive adjective, it is not capitalized.

> My aunt gave me a big hug when I told her the news.
> The brother of my friend has gone to Peru.

Capitalize all words referring to supreme beings and religious scriptures.

> Jehovah   the Bible
> Buddha   the Koran
> Allah   the Bhagavad Gita
> God   the Torah

Capitalize the names of races, languages, nationalities, and religions and any adjectives formed from these names.

> Cree   French   Catholicism   Inuit
> Hinduism   Peruvian   African   Canadian

Looking at Words

Ever wonder why I is capitalized? It isn't a matter of being more important than you. Originally I was written in lower case, but early printers had difficulty setting the word; it would run together with the words before or after it. Their solution was to capitalize I to make it stand out as a whole word.

Exception

Do not capitalize the word god when it is in the plural, or when it refers to one of many gods, such as the gods of ancient Greece and Rome.

Poseidon, the god of the seas

Exercise 1   *Capitalization*

Rewrite these sentences, correcting any capitalization errors.

1. For some reason, it seems europeans have always been fascinated by tibet; i know my parisian uncle, doctor louis st cyr, loves to read about it.

2. Tibet is an isolated, mountain region in the southwest of china; it is situated on a large, high plateau between the kunlun mountains and the himalayas.

3. Before the chinese invasion in 1951, the tibetan people were followers of buddha and practised a unique form of buddhism; now, their spiritual and political leader, the dalai lama, lives in exile in india, and the monasteries are closed.

4. Until recently, the land was inaccessible to non-tibetans due to tibetan and chinese government policies.

5. Now that outsiders are allowed to visit, i'll bet that uncle louis and aunt justine will want to go.

In geographical names, capitalize the first letter of each word, except articles and prepositions.

Continents	North America	Europe
Bodies of Water	the North Sea	Lake Winnipeg
Landforms	the Ural Mountains	Death Valley
World Regions	Central America	the Yukon
Public Areas	Old Faithful	Red Square

Capitalize names of regions of a country or the world, and any adjectives that come from those names.

> the Maritimes/the Maritime provinces
>
> the East/the East Coast
>
> the Prairies/the Prairie provinces
>
> Provence/the Provençal region of France

Do not capitalize compass directions or words that merely indicate direction or a general location.

> The birds fly south in October.
>
> The wheat grew tall on the prairie.
>
> We drove down the east coast all the way from Saint John, New Brunswick to Providence, Rhode Island.

Exercise 2   *Trivia Quiz I*

See how many of these questions you can answer without looking at the answers. Check your guesses with the answers at the bottom of the page, and then rewrite each sentence, filling in the blanks and correcting any capitalization errors. (Be careful: the errors can occur anywhere in the sentence.)

1. The tallest freestanding structure in the world is the _____ , which stands in the south end of the city of _____.

2. Off the east coast, you will find the largest island in north amcrica, _____.

3. The west holds the record for the largest shopping centre in the world, which is the _____ in the province of _____!

4. If you have ever lived in the north, you know that the largest bay in the world is _____.

5. The largest ocean in the world is the _____.

6. The highest mountain in the world is _____ in the eastern _____.

7. The largest desert is the _____ in north _____.

8. The smallest continent in the world is _____.

9. The country with the highest population is _____.

10. The longest rivers in the world are the _____ and the _____.

Answers

1. cn tower, toronto 2. newfoundland 3. west edmonton mall, alberta 4. hudson bay 5. pacific ocean 6. mount everest, himalayas 7. sahara, africa 8. australia 9. china 10. nile, amazon

Capitalize the names of organizations and institutions and their abbreviations.

> New Democratic Party
> United Nations/UN
> Marc Garneau Collegiate Institute

Capitalize the names of historical events, documents, and periods of time.

> Korean War   Charter of Rights
> Middle Ages   Battle of Lundy's Lane

Capitalize the names of months, days, and holidays but not the names of seasons.

> May   Friday   Thanksgiving Day   spring

Exercise 3   *Trivia Quiz II*

See how many of these questions you can answer before you look at the answers at the bottom of the page. Check your score, then rewrite each sentence, filling in the blanks and correcting any capitalization errors.

1. The battle of the plains of _____ took place on september 13, 1759.

2. The oneida, mohawk, onondaga, cayuga, seneca, and tuscarora make up the _____ confederacy.

3. People who follow the religion of islam are called _____ .

4. Most canadians switch to daylight savings time in the _____ .

5. NATO stands for the _____ .

Answers

1. abraham 2. six nations, or *iroquois 3. moslems,* or *muslims 4. spring*
5. north atlantic treaty organization

Capitalize the titles of specific school courses and courses that are followed by a number. School subjects that are languages are always capitalized. *Do not* capitalize the names of school grades or the general names of school subjects.

> grade ten   geometry
> Russian   Introduction to Sociology

Capitalize the names of specific monuments, bridges, and buildings.

> the **L**ions **G**ate **B**ridge
> the **C**algary **S**addle **D**ome
> the **H**alifax **C**itadel

Capitalize the names of the planets in the solar system and other objects in the universe, except words like *sun* and *moon*.

> the eclipsed sun   **J**upiter   **O**rion

Capitalize the word *earth* only when it is used in conjunction with the names of other planets. The word *earth* is not capitalized when the article *the* precedes it.

The earth is the third planet away from the sun in our solar system.
Venus is the planet closest to Earth.

Capitalize date abbreviations *B.C., A.D.; B.C.E., C.E.*

> Cleopatra was born in 69 B.C. (*or* 69 B.C.E.)

Exercise 4   *Capitalization*

Rewrite the following sentences, correcting any errors in capitalization.

1. I registered for ancient history I, business math II, social studies, english, and music.

2. This Thursday at 10:00 a.m., my history teacher is coming to talk to our english class about Julius Caesar, before we start studying the shakespearean play.

3. I already know that Julius Caesar was assassinated in 44 b.c.

4. Shakespeare chose to set the date as the ides of March, or March 15th.

5. He probably chose that date because March, like the planet mars, is named after the roman god of war.

Your Choice

The time abbreviations "A.M." and "P.M." can be capitalized or written in lower case ("a.m." and "p.m.").

Our school day ends at 3:10 P.M. (or 3:10 p.m.).

Neologisms

Neologisms (pronounced nē-OL-o-jizms) are new words that are being added to the language daily. In times of great technological and scientific change, many neologisms spring up. For example...

compuphobia fear of computers

ecocide destruction of the environment by pollutants

futurologist someone who predicts the future based on present trends

mole a spy

downsizing laying off workers and cutting back operations (in a business)

electronic cottage a home office linked to a larger company through computers, faxes, etc.

Generation X the generation after the baby boom (people who were born after 1960)

photoradar cameras that take pictures of speeding cars so that police can issue a ticket

robotics using machines in a factory to do the work formerly done by humans

biodegradable readily decomposed by living microorganisms

Watch for other neologisms being used in newspapers and magazines and on television.

Capitalize the first word of every sentence.

> After six silent years, the child spoke one word.

In general, capitalize the first word of every line of poetry. (In some modern poetry, lines do not begin with a capital letter.)

Canadian student Jan Krasnodebski wrote the following short poem:

> It surely isn't a crime
> To write a poem that doesn't rhyme.

Capitalize the first word of a direct quotation.

> Danny Gallivan coined the phrase, "He shoots, he scores!"

In business and personal letters, capitalize the first word in the greeting; also capitalize the title, the person's name, and words such as *Sir* and *Madam*. Capitalize the first word in the complimentary close.

> Dear Sir or Madam.   Dearest Snookums,
> Sincerely   Yours truly,

Capitalize the first word, the last word, and all other important words in titles. Do not capitalize conjunctions, articles, or prepositions with fewer than five letters.

Book Title	*Such a Long Journey*
Short Story	"A Company of Laughing Faces"
Newspaper	*The Globe and Mail*
Song	"O Canada"
Play	*Amigo's Blue Guitar*
Work of Art	the *Mona Lisa*
Television Series	*The Kids in the Hall*

Exercise 5   *Capitalization*

Rewrite the following letter, inserting capitals as necessary.

r.r. #3,
scofield, b.c.
v6c 6c3
(604) 763 2425

dear severn cullis-suzuki:

I am a grade 9 student at scofield secondary school, and I am writing to tell you how much I enjoyed reading the speech you gave at the Earth Summit in rio centro, brazil. You and your friends in the environmental children's organization have inspired my friends and me to do something in our own high school to help the environment. I think you spoke for all young people when you said, "you are deciding what kind of world we will grow up in." I hope the delegates listened to you.

I am looking forward to reading your new book, *tell the world*. I'm sure it will be full of good ideas. I saw it reviewed in our local paper, the *sentinel*, but it hasn't shown up in the bookstores yet. My brother said that he would buy it for me for my birthday, which is on may 28.

I am enclosing a copy of *earthwatch*, which is a magazine my friends and I produce and circulate around our school. We would like very much to interview you for our next edition. Is there any chance you would be free to talk to me on the phone for fifteen minutes or so in early june? Please let me know as soon as possible.

sincerely yours,

stella sarmazian

Peerless Peer Editing

Here are some guidelines you can use for editing your own writing, or when you are asked to check someone else's writing.

1. **INTRODUCTION**

   - Does it give you a good idea of what to expect in the rest of the essay?
   - Is it interesting? Does it catch your attention?
   - After reading the introduction, can you state the main point of the essay?

2. **PARAGRAPHS**

   - Are the paragraphs clear and interesting?
   - Are they well developed? Mark those that are not.
   - Does each paragraph focus on a single topic?

3. **WORDS**

   - Highlight up to five words that are particularly effective.
   - Highlight five words that are confusing or unclear.

4. **ORGANIZATION**

   - List the main points of each paragraph, in order of presentation.
   - Is there a clear logic to the order of the points?
   - Is there any unnecessary material?
   - Are the transitions smooth and logical?

5. **CONCLUSION**

   - Does the conclusion tie the ideas in the essay together?
   - Does it leave a strong, interesting impression of the essay's thesis?
   - Does it close the essay effectively? or is it too abrupt?

6. **AFTER READING THE WHOLE ESSAY, GO BACK TO THE INTRODUCTION**

   - Does the essay deliver what the introduction promises?
   - Is the thesis well developed and argued in the essay?

Beware!

"No passion in the world is equal to the passion to alter someone else's draft."

H.G. Wells

Editing Marks

$\wedge$ = insert (schöl)

= new paragraph (# Then...)

γ = delete (amused)

$\equiv$ = capital letter (she saw)

/ = lower case (Ðollars)

$\frown$ = close up (did not go)

$\sim$ = transpose (were we)

Punctuation

The Point of Punctuation

1. You shall go to war. You shall return never. In war you shall perish.
2. You shall go to war. You shall return. Never, in war, shall you perish.

When reading a story in a book, you probably pay little attention to the punctuation used. If that punctuation were missing, however, reading would be a struggle. Consider this passage from Jean Mills's novel *The Legacy*, without the original punctuation.

> Is that what you think Anna hissed She wanted to grab him by the shirt and wipe that arrogant sneer off his face Do you think I wanted to come here Walk in among a bunch of strangers and just make myself at home Well youre wrong Anna was furious Id rather be home with my father and my friends

As you can see, punctuation marks are essential. They are signals for a reader. They indicate pauses and show points of emphasis. They tell who is speaking and where ideas begin and end. If you want your readers to understand what you write, you need to use punctuation marks correctly.

Kinds of Punctuation Marks

In this section you will learn how to use the following kinds of punctuation marks:

End marks (. ! ?)	Commas (,)
Semicolons (;)	Colons (:)
Apostrophes (')	Hyphens (-)
Quotation marks (" ")	Underlining (___)

End marks

Use a period at the end of a declarative sentence.

A **declarative sentence** is a sentence that makes a statement. It is the most basic kind of sentence used in writing and for reporting information.

> Palermo is in Sicily.   Two o'clock came and went.

Use a period at the end of an imperative sentence.

An **imperative sentence** is one that requests or orders someone to do something.

> Leave your shoes at the door.   Help me with this.

Use a period at the end of an indirect question.

An **indirect question** tells what someone asked. However, it does not give the exact words of the person who asked the question.

> The diplomat asked whether the government would allow them to leave.

Use a period after most abbreviations and initials.

An **abbreviation** is a shortened form of a word. An initial is a single letter that stands for a word or name.

> Dr. Hannah A. Simon =
> Doctor Hannah Alexandra Simon
>
> Rev. Col. Geo. B. Fee =
> Reverend Colonel George Baxter Fee

Note that a period is not used after a standard, two-letter Canada Post province abbreviation. (See the list on this page.) A period is used after informal province abbreviations, such as Ont., for Ontario, or Alta., for Alberta.

Note that SI unit symbols are not abbreviations and therefore do not require a period.

> km (kilometre)   cm (centimetre)
> g (gram)   s (second)

Common Abbreviations

B.C. (before Christ)
A.D. (of the Christian era)
C.E. (of the common era)
B.C.E. (before the common era)
B.A. (Bachelor of Arts)
M.A. (Master of Arts)
Ph.D. (Doctor of Philosophy)
etc. (and others)
e.g. (for example)
i.e. (that is)

Province and Territory Canada Post Abbreviations

Alberta AB
British Columbia BC
Manitoba MB
New Brunswick NB
Newfoundland and Labrador NF
Northwest Territories NT
Nova Scotia NS
Ontario ON
Quebec PQ
Prince Edward Island PE
Saskatchewan SK
Yukon Territory YT

Acronyms

The word *acronym* comes from the Greek words *akron* (end) and *onoma* (name). Acronyms are words made from the first letters of a group of words. Note: acronyms do not require periods.

laser = **l**ight **a**mplification through **s**timulated **e**mission of **r**adiation
UNESCO = **U**nited **N**ations **E**ducational, **S**cientific, and **C**ultural **O**rganization
radar = **ra**dio **d**etection **a**nd **r**anging
modem = **mo**dulator-**dem**odulator

Now test yourself by guessing what the following acronyms stand for. (Answers are below.)

1.	SONAR	6.	PUPPY
2.	GATT	7.	DINKY
3.	NATO	8.	BURPY
4.	WASP	9.	MUFFY
5.	YUPPY	10.	NIMBY

Answers

1. Sound Navigation and Ranging *2.* General Agreement on Tariffs and Trade *3.* North Atlantic Treaty Organization *4.* White, Anglo-Saxon Protestant *5.* Young Urban Professional *6.* Poor Urban Professional *7.* Double Income No Kids Yet *8.* Bright Unemployed Real Person *9.* Middle-Aged Urban Failure *10.* Not In My Backyard

Initializations

Initializations are letters used as short forms for a phrase. Here are some useful initializations. There is no need to add periods to these. See how many you can guess without looking at the answers.

1. FYI
2. SASE
3. TGIF
4. ASAP
5. VIP
6. TLC

Answers

1. For Your Information 2. Self-Addressed Stamped Envelope 3. Thank Goodness, It's Friday! 4. As Soon As Possible 5. Very Important Person 6. Tender Loving Care

In numerals use a period between dollars and cents and before a decimal.

$18.98   0.853

Use a question mark at the end of an interrogative sentence.

An **interrogative sentence** is one that asks a question.

Does Saturn's moon, Titan, really have geysers on it?

The previous sentence gives the exact words of the person who is asking the question. It is called a **direct question**. A question mark is used only with a direct question.

Use an exclamation point at the end of an exclamatory sentence.

How great that looks!

Use an exclamation point after an interjection or after any other exclamatory expression.

Wow!   Hurrah!   Ugh!   Kapow!

Reminder

An interjection is a word or group of words used to express strong feeling. It may be a real word or simply a group of letters used to represent a sound. It is one of the eight parts of speech.

Exercise 1   *End Marks*

Rewrite the following items, adding the necessary punctuation.

1. Look Up in the sky It's a bird, it's a plane, it's… Superman

2. Have you been in a comic book store lately

3. If you haven't, look out

4. I was in one recently, and I asked the sales clerk if they carried any old Superman comics

5. She looked up sullenly from her portable CD player and pointed to the back of the store

6. I stood there browsing for a long time, until the clerk called out, "Are you planning on buying anything"

7. Hey No one treats me, B J Klevering, like that

8. I looked her straight in the eye, straightened my rumpled collar, and asked, "Would you mind ringing in these two comics while I choose another"

9. At the cash, she said, "That will be $5323 Would you like a bag"

10. Yikes Unfortunately, I was too proud to back down, so if anyone wants to buy a vintage Superman Doomsday comic, please write to me at 7 Mill St, apt 401, Mtl, PQ H2W 1C4

Commas

Use a comma after every item in a series except the last. A series consists of three or more words, phrases, or clauses.

Words   The British flag is red, white, and blue.

Phrases   The dog ran out the door, down the steps, and across the lawn.

Clauses   How baboons forage for food, establish leadership, and find mates are all explained in this book.

Commas are not needed when all the items in a series are joined by *and*, *or*, or *nor*.

> Rain nor sleet nor dark of night...

Use commas after the adverbs *first*, *second*, *third*, and so on, when these adverbs introduce parallel items in a series.

> There are three ways to get good grades: first, pay attention; second, take notes; and third, study.

Use commas between two or more adjectives of equal rank that modify the same noun.

> They drove away in a bright, shiny, expensive car.

Quick Tip

To decide whether adjectives are of equal rank, try placing the word *and* between them. If the *and* sounds natural and if you can reverse the order of the adjectives without changing the meaning, then a comma is needed.

Use a comma to separate an introductory word, phrase, or clause from the rest of the sentence.

> Yes, the ozone layer does protect us from the harmful ultraviolet rays of the sun.

> However, the ozone layer does not block all the sun's ultraviolet rays.

> On hot summer days, many people get sunburned.

> When you go out into the sunshine, you may have to wear sunblock.

The comma may be left out if there would be little pause in speaking.

> At first the sunshine simply feels good on the skin. Then the burning begins.

Use commas to set off words or groups of words that interrupt the flow of thought in a sentence.

Some common interrupters are *however, I suppose, I think, I believe, to tell the truth, nevertheless, by the way, fortunately, on the one hand*, and *in contrast*.

> *Grimm's Fairy Tales* is, to tell the truth, too scary for young children. Some of the tales, moreover, contain stereotyping of men and women.

Interrupted: This matter is, I believe, too important to ignore.

Uninterrupted: I believe this matter is too important to ignore.

Interrupted: I have, however, had little luck in finding anyone who is willing to help.

Uninterrupted: However, I have had little luck in finding anyone who is willing to help.

Writing Tips

Interrupting your sentences will tend to reduce the impact of what you say. Sometimes, that might be just what you want. However, for maximum impact, try placing the group of words at the beginning of the sentence.

Exercise 2   *Commas and End Marks*

Rewrite the following sentences, adding the necessary punctuation.

1. Theatresports as its name suggests is part theatre and part sports

2. It is another name for improvisational comedy or improv for short

3. While the idea originated in Calgary in 1977 there are now groups in Calgary Toronto Halifax and Vancouver as well as in countries around the world

4. Here is how it works: first players divide into two teams; second they ask the audience for a word phrase or sentence to start the game off; third each team steps out on stage and starts to improvise

5. Although a panel of judges decides which team is the winner the audience can make its feelings known by laughing yelling and throwing foam-rubber boo-bricks

6. Anything can happen at a Theatresports performance: when we went a man in the audience lost his head jumped up on stage and started yodelling

7. However the players didn't miss a beat: they simply incorporated the yodeller into their skit

8. Yes some skits bomb completely and some go on too long but some are just hilarious

9. A lot of successful well-established comedians including Martin Short and The Kids in the Hall began their careers with Theatresports

10. Remember Theatresports often runs workshops on improv for the public so you too can discover your hidden talent as a comedian

Use commas to set off nouns of direct address.

The name of someone directly spoken to is a noun of **direct address**.

> If you look through the microscope, Pina, you'll see the round, green chloroplasts.

> Najma, you won the election!

Use commas to set off the speaker's tags used with direct quotations.

When you repeat someone's exact words, you make a **direct quotation**. A direct quotation is usually accompanied by explanatory words known as **speaker's tags**. Examples of speaker's tags include *Tina said, Gemma answered*, and *Xavier asked*.

> The pilot said, "We shall land in approximately twenty-three minutes."

> "We shall land in approximately twenty-three minutes," the pilot said.

> "We shall land," the pilot said, "in approximately twenty-three minutes."

Croakers

Can you spot the puns in these speaker's tags?

"We've taken over the government," the general cooed.

"You can't really train a beagle," he dogmatized.

"That's no beagle, that's a mongrel," she muttered.

"You ought to see a psychiatrist," she reminded me.

"That's my gold mine!" he claimed.

Say It Again, Sam...

Speaker's tags can reveal a great deal about the speaker's state of mind and tone of voice. Consider how changing the verb in the speaker's tag alters the mood of the following sentence.

"You make me laugh," she said/she snarled/she giggled/she howled.
(*Said* gets the message across, but *giggled* creates a whole scene in your head.)

You don't need to use the same speaker's tag over and over in your writing. The possibilities are endless. Think of as many synonyms (words with similar meaning) for *say* as you can for each of the following categories:

to say softly	to say loudly	to say angrily or unhappily
whisper	thunder	hiss
murmur	bawl	groan

Do not use commas with indirect quotations.

> The pilot said that the plane would land in a few minutes.

Use a comma before the conjunction that joins the two main clauses in a compound sentence.

> Kaori seemed to agree, and no one else objected.

Quick Tip

Make sure that the two parts being joined are, indeed, complete clauses. A comma is not needed to separate compound predicates.

Compound Predicate Sal turned on the radio and sat down to listen to it.
Compound Sentence Sal turned on the radio, and then he sat down to listen to it.

Exercise 3 *Commas*

Rewrite the following sentences, adding commas where needed. If no comma is needed, write "correct."

1. If you must insult someone do it with style.

2. There is a fine art to battling someone with words and you would do well to learn from the masters.

3. In ancient Greece the statesman Demosthenes once told one of his enemies Phocion that the citizens of Athens would kill him one day when they were in a rage.

4. "And you when they are in their senses" replied Phocion.

5. "You little pipsqueak" an angry voter once yelled at former Saskatchewan Premier Tommy Douglas "I could swallow you in one bite."

6. "And if you did my friend you'd have more brains in your belly than you have in your head" quipped Douglas.

7. Groucho Marx the famous comedian once said "I've had a wonderful evening but this wasn't it."

8. It was Groucho who resigned his membership in an exclusive club because he didn't want to belong to any club that would accept him as a member.

9. Dorothy Parker a critic and author wrote in a book review "This is not a book to be tossed aside lightly; it should be thrown with great force."

10. Finally someone once described journalist Clifford Makins as "A legend in his own lunchtime."

In dates, use a comma between the day of the week, the day of the month, and the year.

> Friday, October 15, 1993   July 1, 1867

However, no commas are necessary when the following styles are used.

> July 1992   3 June 1993

Use a comma between the name of a city or town and the name of a province, state, or country.

> Surprise, British Columbia   Frankfurt, Germany

In writing an address as part of a sentence, use a comma after each item. (Note that you do not place a comma between the province and the postal code.)

> Please forward our mail to 651 Sentinel Drive, Richmond Hill, Ontario L4C 3Z7.

Use a comma after the salutation of a friendly letter and after the complimentary close of a friendly letter or a business letter.

> Dear Tim,   Yours sincerely,

Use a comma when there is danger of misreading or confusion if a comma is not used.

> Who she is, is a mystery.   Inside, it was warm.

Reminder

If a date is used to introduce a sentence, follow the rule for introductory words or phrases, and put a comma after the year:

On January 1, 2001, we begin a new millenium.

That What?

Try using punctuation (commas, capitals, question marks, and periods) to make the following group of words make sense. (The answer is below.)

that that is is that that is not is not is not that it

Answer

That that is, is. That that is not, is not. Is not that it?

Exercise 4   *Commas*

Rewrite the following letters, adding commas where necessary.

Friday October 14 1994

Dear Myra
Would you please send me the Shums's new address? Somehow I've managed to lose the piece of paper Allan gave me that contained all the information about their move. I can't imagine what I did with it but wherever it's gone gone it is. I'd appreciate any help you can give me.

Your friend

Theo

Wednesday October 19 1994

Dear Theo

I'm happy to give you what information I have about the Shums's address. Unfortunately it isn't very accurate. Lydia left me a note with her new address before she left but she was in a hurry and her handwriting is hard to read. I know it says Church Street; the question is is that a 1 or a 7 in their street number? Seven I'd say but don't hold me to it. The note says: As of October 10 1994 our new address is (1 or 7?) Church St. Nanaimo BC V6C 1E5.

Let me know if you have any luck. I know Allan will be anxious to hear from you.

Your friend

Myra

Exercise 5   *End Mark and Comma Review*

Rewrite the following letter, adding periods, question marks, exclamation points, and commas as necessary.

Mr Raffi Armenian
RR1
Sioux Lookout Ont
M6Y 2Y5

Monday June 6 1994

Dear Raffi

I just thought I'd drop you a line to let you know we got home safely and that we really enjoyed seeing you for the weekend Thanks for your hospitality.

Raffi remember when you said those country roads could be scary at night How right you were We had quite an adventure on the way home At about 10:00 p.m. we were all telling scary stories when the car got a flat tire It was dark of course and we didn't have a flashlight Nevertheless Reza Nish and I all clambered out and started fumbling around; since the car belonged to Reza's dad we weren't sure where the jack was No one paid much attention to Mickey our Old English Sheepdog

The moon was full but the trees on both sides of the road were so dense it seemed almost pitch black Suddenly there was a movement of branches and a strange figure appeared from the trees With the moon behind it it looked like something from the planet Mars with spikes all over and two antennae on its head

So what did we do First we gasped; second we screamed; and third we ran like blazes Nish stopped running first because her shoe fell off She looked back sniffed and then started laughing "Here boy" she called and the creature started slinking toward us

Of course it was Mickey who had wandered off into the woods and rolled in something old dead and very smelly Some branches had stuck in his hair and that was what had looked at least to our impressionable minds like antennae He was so ashamed of himself he stayed perfectly quiet and didn't even try to chase us

Once the tire was on we got out of there as fast as we could and we sang rousing songs the rest of the way home to keep our minds off the dark and aliens Unfortunately we had to drive with the windows open and Mickey lying morosely in the hatchback We aired the car out overnight and sprayed it with air freshener but Reza's dad still asked what we had done to leave such an awful smell

Talk to you soon I hope If you feel like dropping me a line my address is 1041 Macmillan Ave Winnipeg MB O1O 3G2.

Your friend

Sami

PS Mickey by the way is now clean as a whistle and he promises never to wander into the woods again

Semicolons

A **semicolon** separates sentence elements. It indicates a more definite break than a comma does but a less abrupt break than a period does.

Use a semicolon to join the two parts of a compound sentence if no coordinating conjunction is used.

Remember that a semicolon may be used only if the clauses are closely related.

> Julia has finished reading the assignment; Ben has not yet begun.

Use a semicolon before a conjunctive adverb that joins the clauses of a compound sentence.

A **conjunctive adverb** is a word such as *therefore* or *however* that shows a relationship between two clauses. Note that a comma should **not** be used before conjunctive adverbs.

Incorrect:	The race was long and difficult, however, everyone in our group managed to finish.
Correct:	The race was long and difficult; however, everyone in our group managed to finish.

Use a semicolon to separate the items of a series if one or more of these items contain commas.

> I have lived in these places: Love, Saskatchewan; Bumble Bee, Arizona; Dingo, Australia; and Cheddar, England.

Colons

Use a colon to introduce a list of items.

A word or phrase such as *these* or *the following* is often followed by a **colon.** A colon must be preceded by an independent clause and not used directly after a preposition or a verb.

> You will need the following items when you arrive at camp: a sleeping bag, a flashlight, and a tennis racquet.

Use a colon to introduce a long or formal quotation.

> In her memoirs, columnist Marjorie Nichols wrote: The role of the press used to be to provide a check on excessive political power, but now it's gone the other way. The genuine power to influence now rests with television, not the politicians.

Use a colon between two principal clauses when the second clause explains the first.

The first word following a colon is not capitalized unless it is a proper noun or the start of a quotation.

> Moses Znaimer knows about broadcasting: he has been in the business since 1965.

Use a colon after the greeting in a formal letter.

> Dear Sir or Madam: Dear Professor Pavlicek:

Use a colon between numbers showing hours and minutes.

> 7:30 p.m.   12:00 noon

Hyphens

Use a hyphen between syllables divided at the end of a line.

> Have you read the Canadian Con-
> stitution?

Use a hyphen in compound numbers from twenty-one to ninety-nine. Use a hyphen in fractions.

> eighty-three   one-fifth
> forty-five   eight thirds

Use a hyphen in certain compound nouns.

> sister-in-law   self-respect

Use a hyphen between the words that make up a compound adjective when the modifier is used before a noun.

> self-conscious people   well-known commentator

Do not use a hyphen between adverbs ending in *-ly* and adjectives when used before nouns.

> nearly new car

Hyphenating at the End of a Line

1. Divide a word only between syllables.
2. Hyphenate only words of two or more syllables.
3. Make sure that at least two letters of the word fall on each line.

Writing Tip

A covering letter such as this one should above all be informative. Keep your sentences short and to the point, use as many strong verbs as you can, avoid the passive voice, and describe your most impressive qualifications first. Can you suggest any ways to improve Ewan's letter?

Exercise 6   *Semicolons, Colons, and Hyphens*

Rewrite the following letter, adding semicolons, colons, and hyphens as needed.

Ewan Atto
165 Concord Ave
Toronto, ON M6T 2G5

Mr. Gary Wijngaard
Personnel Director, Camp Wombat
P.O. Box 24 Station C
Oakwood, AB
T3G 1B1

Dear Sir

I am writing to apply for the position of Senior Counsellor at Camp Wombat, which was advertised on the bulletin board at my school. My qualifications for this position include the follow ing three summers' experience, first as a camper and then as a junior counsellor, at Camp Chachabonga a love of sports and well developed leadership skills.

My three years at Camp Chachabonga taught me a lot about leadership and responsibility as a junior counsellor I was res ponsible for ten campers ranging in age from 7 to 9 years old. The camp catered to both able bodied campers and those with physical disabilities one third of all the campers were in wheel chairs, including three of my charges.

I learned another important skill at Chachabonga self discipline. When you are in charge of rousing ten sleepy campers from their beds at 5 00 a.m. to go hiking, you need lots of self discipline!

I would greatly enjoy working as a Senior Counsellor at Camp Wombat this summer moreover, I believe I have a lot to offer both the campers and the other staff members enthusiasm, effort, and a sense of fun!

I have attached a copy of my résumé. Please feel free to call me to arrange an interview. I look forward to meeting you.

Yours sincerely,

Ewan Atto

Apostrophes

Use an apostrophe to form the possessive of singular and plural nouns. To form the possessive of a singular noun, add an apostrophe and -*s*, even if the noun ends in -*s*.

> Carlos's book   the bank's entrance

To form the possessive of a plural noun that ends in -*s*, add an apostrophe only. To form the possessive of a plural noun that does not end in -*s*, add both an apostrophe and -*s*.

> the girls' bicycles   the men's stories
> mice's tails   the people's choice

Use an apostrophe in a contraction to show where one or more letters have been left out. Avoid using contractions in formal writing.

> can't = *cannot*   he'll = *he will* or *he shall*
> I've = *I have*   Mico's = *Mico is* or *Mico has*

Use an apostrophe to show the omission of figures in a date.

> the winter of '75   the class of '96

Use an apostrophe to show the plurals of letters, numbers, signs, and words referred to as words.

> There are two *r*'s and two *s*'s in the word *embarrassment*.

> There are too many *and*'s in that sentence.

Exercise 7   *Apostrophes*

Rewrite the following sentences, adding apostrophes as needed.

1. There are two ss in the word "dessert" when it refers to sweets eaten after a meal.

2. Thats easy for me to remember, because there are two words in my favourite desserts name: ice cream.

3. Did you know that Häagen Dazss name is made up?

4. Its not from Scandinavia; its birthplace is the Bronx!

Other Uses of Apostrophes

Apostrophes are also used to show omitted letters in dialect, old-fashioned speech, or poetry.

'Twas the night before Christmas.

'Tis me own t'ing, man.

5. Häagen Dazss creators name is Bill Mattus, but hes since sold the company to Pillsbury.

6. Heres another piece of ice cream trivia: ice cream sundaes got their name because, back in the 90s of the last century, it was considered wrong to sip sodas on Sundays.

7. The soda fountain owners response was to concoct an ice cream dish without the soda, and sundaes were born.

8. Canadians feelings toward ice cream are made clear by the fact that we are the fourth largest consumers of ice cream in the world.

9. Ice cream may not be everyones favourite, but I dont know anyone who cant stand it.

10. Its certainly popular at childrens parties!

Quotation Marks and Underlining

Use quotation marks to begin and end a direct quotation.

> Sonja said, "My feelings are hurt."

Do not use quotation marks to set off an indirect quotation. Indirect quotations are often signalled by the word *that*.

> Sonja said that her feelings were hurt.

To punctuate a direct quotation, enclose the exact words used by a speaker or writer in quotation marks. Capitalize the first word of the quotation, and place commas inside the quotation marks. When the end of the quotation falls at the end of the sentence, place the period inside the quotation marks.

> The butler said, "The Mayor is here to see you."
>
> "Kilroy was here," read the writing on the wall.

Put question marks and exclamation marks inside the quotation marks if they are part of the quotation.

> "How deep is the mid-Atlantic trench?" asked Ayelet.
>
> "Help!" cried the shepherd. "There's a wolf circling my flock!"

Put question marks and exclamation marks outside the quotation marks if they are not part of the quotation.

Was it Marshall McLuhan who said, "The medium is the message"?

Always put commas and periods inside the quotation marks.

The president of the World Bank said, "We now understand the importance of preserving the rain forest."

"We now understand the importance of preserving the rain forest," the president of the World Bank said.

Enclose the parts of a divided quotation in quotation marks. Do not capitalize the first word of the second part unless it begins a new sentence.

"I'd rather play chamber music," said Linda Hecker, "than go to a party or a movie."

"Our standard of living is rising," said the foreign minister of Zimbabwe. "However, we are now facing an ecological crisis."

In punctuating dialogue, begin a new paragraph to indicate a new speaker.

"Nothing wrong with my heart," said Lionel. "It's my tonsils that hurt."

"You don't have to worry," said the nurse. "A heart operation like yours is really very simple."

"My heart is just fine."

"And it'll be even better tomorrow."

from Green Grass, Running Water *by Thomas King*

When quoting passages longer than one paragraph, use quotation marks at the beginning of each paragraph and at the end of only the last paragraph.

Here's what Ian Hanomansing, a CBC television reporter, has to say about his job:

"If the story is finished and I can be in the studio when the piece is being edited, I'll start off by screening all the pictures and all the interviews again. If

Citing Your Sources

For information on documenting sources of quotations, see Appendix A, "Research and Writing."

Alternative

Instead of putting quotation marks at the beginning of each paragraph of a quotation, you may wish to set it off from the surrounding text by indenting the whole quotation. Don't indent and use quotation marks, though.

I come back with three tapes, I will know in advance that there wil be a lot of material to get through.

"I usually know that I want to start the story with certain pictures, then go to another sequence. We film in sequences; that is, a series of shorts of a certain piece of action. The person who will edit the tape is screening along with me, looking at the pictures as well."

Use quotation marks to enclose the titles of short stories, poems, essays, magazine and newspaper articles, chapters, television episodes, and songs.

Short Story	"Just Lather, That's All"
Poem	"The Bull Moose"
Essay	"Urban Legends"
Magazine or Newspaper Article	"Killer Blizzard Strikes"
Chapter	Chapter 1, "My Early Life"
Television Episode	"The Trouble with Tribbles"
Song	"Universal Soldier"

The titles of books, newspapers, magazines, movies, television series, plays, works of art, and long musical compositions are <u>underlined</u> in writing and *italicized* in print.

Book	*Little by Little*
Newspaper	*Halifax Chronicle-Herald*
Magazine	*Maclean's*
Movie	*My American Cousin*
Television Series	*The Nature of Things*
Play	*A Midsummer Night's Dream*
Work of Art	Emily Carr's *Big Raven*
Musical Composition	Wagner's *The Ring*

Exercise 8   *Quotation Marks and Underlining*

Rewrite the following sentences, adding quotation marks or underlining as necessary.

1. The school newspaper, the Bugle, is going to print an article I wrote, entitled Famous Last Words, which is all about great endings of one sort or another.

2. Probably the most famous last line of all is the one found in stories such as Cinderella and Rapunzel.

3. It goes, And they lived happily ever after.

4. In film, the best-loved ending must be that of Casablanca.

5. Louis, says Rick, I think this is the beginning of a beautiful friendship.

6. On the other hand, for sheer terror, I'd nominate the final scene in the Donald Sutherland version of Invasion of the Body Snatchers.

7. The television series The Prisoner is a classic, with a real surprise ending.

8. You should try to get it on video; the final episode is called Fallout, but to appreciate the twist, watch them all from the beginning.

9. I'm glad that the film Gone with the Wind kept the same last line as Margaret Mitchell's book.

10. Who can forget Vivien Leigh's final line, After all, tomorrow is another day?

Research and Writing

Research is looking for facts or truth—an inquiry or investigation.

- **Primary Research** is investigating a topic first-hand; for example, through interviews or surveys.
- **Secondary Research** is finding facts and evidence in books, articles, computer on-line services, and videos.

Finding Facts: The Dewey Decimal System

In the library, books and other materials are organized according to a system of numbers and letters. *Water Monsters*, for example, has the number 011.944 GAR. The main groups in the system are:

100—Philosophy	600—Technology
200—Religion	700—Fine Arts
300—Social Sciences	800—Literature
400—Language	900—History and Geography
500—Science	

Check your library for more information on the Dewey decimal system.

The Shape of a Research Paper

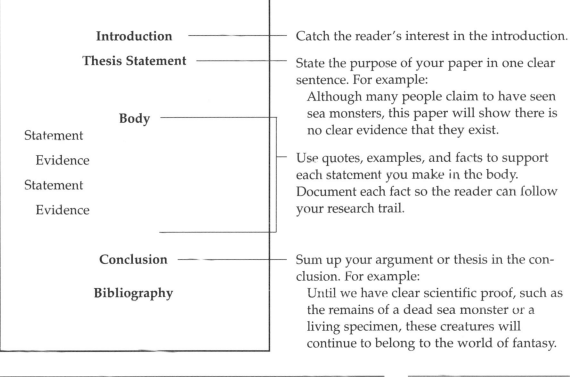

Introduction ———————— Catch the reader's interest in the introduction.

Thesis Statement ———————— State the purpose of your paper in one clear sentence. For example:

> Although many people claim to have seen sea monsters, this paper will show there is no clear evidence that they exist.

Body

Statement

Evidence

Statement

Evidence

Use quotes, examples, and facts to support each statement you make in the body. Document each fact so the reader can follow your research trail.

Conclusion ———————— Sum up your argument or thesis in the conclusion. For example:

> Until we have clear scientific proof, such as the remains of a dead sea monster or a living specimen, these creatures will continue to belong to the world of fantasy.

Bibliography

Seven Steps to Success

Tackle a research paper step-by-step.

Step 1. Select your **topic**.

Step 2. Make a quick skeleton **outline** of what you want to say.

Step 3. Narrow your **focus**—write your thesis statement.

Step 4. Select **evidence:** a) primary
b) secondary

Step 5. **Document** your evidence.

Step 6. First **draft**.

Step 7. **Revise** and edit—final draft.

Research Tip

When you look for information in a book, first check the publication information to see if it is current. Then check the Table of Contents and Index to make sure that what you need is there. If so, skim the appropriate section or chapter before reading it in detail to make sure it is relevant to your topic. This way, you can check out many books in a short time.

Title Page

Title pages usually include:

> Topic
> Name
> Class
>
>
> Submitted to:
> For: (course or
>   subject)
> Date:

Using Quotations

If you quote material directly from a book or magazine in the body of your paper, reproduce it carefully so that it's exactly as it appears in the original, including spelling, punctuation, and paragraphs.

Short Quotes

If the quote is less than three lines, just use quotation marks and run it into the text. For example:

> In the summer of 1855, the local paper claimed that reports of sightings "have attracted to this village many of the citizens of the adjoining towns and villages (Garinger, 47)." Business had never been better in the little town of Perry.

Longer Quotes

If the quote is more than three lines long, you need to set your quote off from the main body of your paper:

- indent four spaces
- use single spacing for the quoted material
- don't use quotation marks. For example:

> The Silver Lake monster was proved to be a very clever hoax. In 1857 the Walker House Hotel in Perry burned to the ground. In the charred ruins workers found the burned remains of "the monster."
>
> > The canvas body was painted a deep green with bright yellow spots to give it a grotesque appearance. The bright red eyes and mouth suggested a fearsome creature. A series of weights along the edge of the canvas caused the structure to sink into the water, and long ropes attached to strategic parts allowed the conspirators to operate it like a gigantic marionette. (Garinger, 50-51)

Cite Your Sources

In order to document a quote, put the author's name and the page number in parentheses after the quote. This is called citing your source.

Short Quotes

Cite after the quotation marks, before the end punctuation.

Longer Quotes

Cite after the end punctuation. Leave two spaces before the brackets. If more than one page is cited, separate the numbers with a hyphen.

Quotes with No Author

If your article is from an encyclopedia or other reference book, give a shortened version of the title and the page number.

List of Works Cited

Your "List of Works Cited" should be a separate page at the end of your paper, just before the bibliography. Put a line space between each entry.

Entry for a signed article in an encyclopedia
Ewing, J.A. "Steam Engines and Other Heat Engines." *Encyclopaedia Britannica*, 9th ed XXII: 473–526.

Entry for a book
Garinger, Alan. *Water Monsters*. San Diego: Greenhaven Press, Inc., 1991: 48–53.

Entry for an unsigned article in a magazine or newspaper
"High-Speed Test Network to Link Regional Nets." *The Computer Paper* June 1994: 80.

Entry for an unsigned article in an encyclopedia
"Sea Snake." *Funk & Wagnall's New Encyclopedia* vol. 23: 270.

Entry for a signed article in a magazine or newspaper
Visser, Margaret. "It's Snowing What to Say." *Saturday Night* Feb. 1994: 30.

Footnote and Endnote Formats

A footnote has four parts: name, title, publication information, and page number. Note the punctuation used; there is only one period at the end. The first line should be indented five spaces.

Books
A. One Author
    1. Cicely Berry, *Voice and the Actor* (London: Harrap, 1979) 21.

B. Two Authors
    2. Owen Beattie and John Geiger, *Frozen in Time: Unlocking the Secrets of the Franklin Expedition* (Saskatoon: Western Producer Prairie Books, 1988) 9.

Magazines, Encyclopedias, Reports, Newspapers
A. Author Named
    3. Susan Pearce, "Training the Family Dog." *Dogs in Canada Annual* 1989: 40.

B. No Author
    4. The Talk of the Town," *The New Yorker*, 30 May 1994: 35.

Another Style: Endnotes and Footnotes

Many people prefer footnotes or endnotes because they don't interrupt the flow of the research paper with citations. Instead of a citation, a number appears above the end of a quote. A footnote appears at the foot or bottom of the page. Endnotes appear at the end of the paper.

Media and Other Sources

A. A Personal Interview
> 5. Tom Hennessey, personal interview, 20 June 1994.

B. A Film or Video
> 6. *The Grapes of Wrath*, dir. John Ford, with John Carradine, Jane Darwell, and Henry Fonda, writ. Nunnally Johnson, Twentieth Century-Fox, 1940.

C. Song Lyrics
> 7. Brad Roberts, "Superman's Song."

The Final Page—Bibliography

A bibliography looks very much like a list of works cited, but without the page numbers included. Your bibliography should list all the books, articles, and other sources you have read or consulted to write your paper. Even if you have not used a quote from a source it is useful to list it. It shows the depth of your research and may help someone else researching the same topic.

Remember:
*   Your bibliography is always arranged alphabetically.
*   The author's last name is first—Jack Jones becomes "Jones, Jack."
*   Indent the second line five spaces.
*   Underline the title of the book or magazine.
*   Each entry has three main parts: name, title, publication information. Each part ends with a period.
*   You don't need page numbers.

For example:

> Berry, Cicely. *Voice and the Actor*. London: Harrap, 1979.

author   title   publication information

A List of Commonly Confused Words

In the list below, you will find groups of words that are often confused. The words are in alphabetical order. If you are not sure which word to use when you are writing, check this list. Check your dictionary for words not in the list.

a
Use *a* before words starting with a consonant sound.
   His appetite is *a* hopeful sign.
an
Use *an* before a word starting with a vowel sound.
   He is *an* honest man.

accept
a verb meaning "receive"
   I *accept* your gift with thanks.
except
a preposition meaning "other than"
   She invited everyone *except* me.
a verb meaning "to take out" or "to leave out"
   Please *except* her from my list.

advice
a noun meaning "help, suggestion"
   She gave me good *advice*.
advise
a verb meaning "to give advice"
   What did you *advise* her to do?

affect
a verb meaning "to influence"
   How did that *affect* you?
effect
a noun meaning "a result"
   What *effect* did that have on you?

allot
a verb meaning "to distribute" or "to assign"
   The teacher *allotted* work to each student
a lot
a great quantity
   He ate *a lot* of ice cream.

all together
everyone together
   Our family is *all together* now.
altogether
completely
   You are *altogether* wrong.

already
by that time, before now
   We had *already* gone.
all ready
everyone ready, completely ready
   Are you *all ready* to go?

alright
This is the non-standard spelling of *all right*.
all right
This is the standard form. It should always be used.
   Is it *all right* for me to be here?

among
Use this word to mean "in the middle of" when you refer to three or more.
   There is a good feeling *among* the members.
between
Use this word to mean "the space or time separating things," usually referring to two items.
   He divided the apple *between* Tom and me.

amount
Use *amount* to refer to things that can be measured.
   He has a large *amount* of candy.
number
Use *number* to refer to things that can be counted.
   There was a large *number* of people at the game.

beside
a preposition meaning "next to"
   He sat *beside* me.
besides
an adverb meaning "in addition to"
   Besides being angry with you, I am also disappointed.

borrow
to take temporarily
   May I *borrow* your rake?
lend
to give temporarily
   Will you *lend* me your rake?

bring
to carry something toward the person speaking
   Bring me that paper.
take
to carry something away from the person speaking
   Will you *take* this to your mother, please?

can
to have the ability
may
to be allowed to, give permission to

capital
location of government
   St. John's is the *capital* of Newfoundland.
money for investment
   I don't have the *capital* to expand the business.
an uppercase letter
   Use a *capital* with proper nouns such as "Parliament."
involving loss of life
   This meaning is usual only in the phrase *capital* punishment.
capitol
U.S. term for the building where legislative assemblies meet
As a proper noun it refers to the building where the U.S. Congress meets in Washington.
   The dome of the *Capitol* rises over Washington; the Illinois state *capitol* can be found in Springfield.

counsel
verb: to give advice
   Did he *counsel* you well?
noun: advice
   He gave me good *counsel*.
council
a group of people who advise
   I belong to the student *council*.

emigrate
to leave a country; use with *from*
  My great-grandparents *emigrated* from
  Ireland.
immigrate
to come into a country; use with *to*
  They *immigrated* to Canada.

farther
Use with distances that can be measured.
  Walk a bit *farther* with me.
further
Use with matters of degree that cannot be
measured.
  Let us study the matter *further*.

fewer
Use with things that can be counted.
  I have *fewer* apples than he has.
less
Use with things that cannot be counted.
  He has *less* ability than she has.

formally
in a formal manner
  She was dressed *formally*.
formerly
previously
  I *formerly* attended that school.

in
within a place
  Jayne was sleeping *in* her room.
into
movement toward an inside place
  Jayne went *into* her room.

its
the possessive pronoun
  The horse hurt *its* foot.
it's
the contraction meaning "it is"
  It's a fine day.

kind, sort
Both these words are singular.
  I like that *kind*.
Do not use *a* after *kind of* or *sort of*.
  This *kind of* tree is subject to disease.
Do not use *kind of* or *sort of* to mean *rather*.
  I am *rather* tired.

learn
to acquire knowledge
  It's easy to *learn* how to spell.
teach
to help someone acquire knowledge
  Teach me how to spell.

leave
to go, to let stay
  The train will *leave* soon.
  Leave the window open.
let
to permit
  Let the dog go.

like
a preposition
  It tastes *like* strawberries.
as
a conjunction
  It tastes *as* it should.

loose
not attached
  The boat is *loose*.
lose
to misplace
  Did you *lose* your money?

maybe
an adverb meaning "perhaps"
  Maybe we'll go to the movies tonight.
may be
a verb phrase
  We *may be* able to go to the movies tonight.

principal
main, most important
  The *principal* factor is our morale.
the head of a school
  The *principal* visited all the classes on
  Monday.
principle
rule or code of conduct
  It was a *principle* of his never to gamble.

respectfully
with respect
  He signed the letter *"respectfully* yours."
respectively
in the order listed
  The first three prizes went to Tom, Sue, and
  Mary, *respectively*.

stationary
not moving
  That sign is *stationary*.
stationery
writing paper
  Use your best *stationery* when you write to
  your grandparents.

their
the possessive pronoun
  They brought *their* books.
there
the adverb meaning "in that place"
  Put it *there*.
they're
the contraction meaning "they are"
  They're good people.

too
also, excessive
  You *too* are invited.
to
in that direction
  He gave it *to* me.
two
the number
  Two of us are eligible.

who's
the contraction meaning "who is"
  Who's your friend?
whose
the possessive
  Whose book is this?

your
the possessive
  She is *your* friend.
you're
the contraction meaning "you are"
  You're wrong about that.

Answers to Exercises

SECTION ONE

Exercise 1 **1.** Gregor *(noun)*, uneasy *(adjective)*, he *(pronoun)*, into *(preposition)* **2.** was *(verb)*, in *(preposition)* **3.** O *(interjection)*, monarchs *(noun)* **4.** so *(conjunction)*, down *(adverb)*, unicorns *(noun)* **5.** delicately *(adverb)*, I *(pronoun)* **6.** and *(conjunction)* **7.** who *(pronoun)*, eat *(verb)* **8.** cries *(noun)*, once *(adverb)* **9.** tawny *(adjective)*, away *(adverb)* **10.** against *(preposition)*, Pacific Maid *(noun)*

SECTION TWO

Exercise 1 **1.** phrase **2.** subordinate clause **3.** *Irina fixed. (principal clause)* **4.** subordinate clause **5.** *It was the seafood. (principal clause)* **6.** phrase **7.** phrase **8.** *Give me a call. (principal clause)* **9.** subordinate clause **10.** *Rehearse your interviewing techniques. (principal clause)*

Exercise 2 **1.** Europe and the United States produce most board games played in Canada. (ss: *Europe and the United States*; sp: *produce*) **2.** One notable exception is the board game called *Trivial Pursuit*. (ss: *exception*; sp: *is*) **3.** This game, which has been extremely successful, was invented by a group of Canadians in the early 1980s. (ss: *game*; sp: *was invented*) **4.** Since then, it has been copied and sold all over the world. (ss: *it*; sp: *has been copied and sold*) **5.** All of the people who originally invested in the game are now millionnaires. (ss: *all*; sp: *are*) **6.** Many versions of the original game are available, aimed at people of different ages and with different interests. (ss: *versions*; sp: *are*) **7.** Each member of a team answers trivia questions and moves a gamepiece around a board. (ss: *member*; sp: *answers and moves*) **8.** Winning or losing is less important than having fun and learning a thing or two! (ss: *winning or losing*; sp: *is*) **9.** We like to take turns asking the questions while everyone else guesses the answers. (ss: *we*; sp: *like*) **10.** Thanks to the success of *Trivial Pursuit*, game inventing is flourishing in Canada. (ss: *inventing*; sp: *is flourishing*)

Exercise 3 Note: Answers may vary. **1.** *Comedians* make people laugh. **2.** *It is hard work to* come up with original gags and funny stories. **3.** Many never make the big time. **4.** *However, young hopefuls still perform every night* in comedy clubs around the country. **5.** After a comedian has appeared on television, *his or her career may take off.* **6.** *Until then, aspiring artists may* attend acting schools or simply learn by watching other comedians. **7.** *By doing so, they learn the* tricks of the trade, such as raising one's voice at the end of a punch line. **8.** Every comic must contend with hecklers. **9.** *Young performers must* learn what to do and say when there are hecklers in the audience. **10.** The best way to deal with a heckler *is to make him or her look foolish.*

Exercise 4 **1.** sentence **2.** sentence *or fragment* **3.** sentence **4.** sentence **5.** fragment **6.** sentence **7.** fragment **8.** sentence **9.** fragment **10.** fragment

Exercise 5 Note: In all cases where colons or semicolons have been indicated, a period, with a capital letter following, would also be correct. **1.** The great period of the Inca empire began when a neighbouring nation threatened to invade Inca land. The Incas met their neighbours on the battlefield and overpowered them. **2.** When they conquered an area, the Incas enlisted its men into their army; *thus* the Inca army grew to mighty proportions. **3.** By the late 1400s the empire was at its height. *Its* ruler was named Huayna Capac. **4.** Huayna Capac had two sons. The older, Huáscar, was supposed to become ruler of the Incas after his father died, but Huayna Capac gave half the empire to the younger son, Atahualpa. **5.** After Huayna Capac died, the two brothers declared war on each other. Each raised an enormous army. **6.** Their battles left thousands of warriors dead. Finally Atahualpa defeated Huáscar for good in a great battle. **7.** While Atahualpa was relaxing at a resort after the battle, he heard a strange report: some odd-looking bearded men had arrived. **8.** The Incas had never seen Europeans before; *they* thought that Francisco Pizarro and his Spanish conquistadors must be gods. **9.** Pizarro captured Atahualpa and held him for ransom. *He* promised to release the Inca king if his subjects would fill a ransom room with gold. **10.** The Incas filled the room with gold; *however,* Pizarro simply took the gold and killed the Inca leader anyway.

Exercise 6 1. fragment 2. fragment 3. run-on 4. run-on 5. run-on 6. run-on 7. run-on 8. sentence **Note: Answers may vary.** Langston Hughes was one of the leading writers of the Harlem Renaissance. He was born in 1902 in Joplin, Missouri, at the beginning of a new century and of a new age in African-American culture. From an early age, he devoured the poetry of Carl Sandburg and Walt Whitman. He himself began publishing poetry at the age of nineteen. Hughes studied at Columbia University. After one year he left school and became a sailor on a freighter. Hughes ended up in Paris; there he listened to jazz in crowded nightclubs. Hughes's first book of poetry was published in 1926. That same year Hughes enrolled at Lincoln University. Hughes's first novel, *Not Without Laughter,* portrayed everyday African-American life. It was a great success. In 1939, he founded the Harlem Suitcase Theater.

Exercise 7 1. The Cambrian period of geology began around 570 million years ago. (sentence) 2. *It* lasted for about 70 million years. (fragment) 3. For millions of years, only very simple life forms such as worms and anemones *existed*. (fragment) 4. Then a huge explosion of animal evolution took place. *In* the space of a mere 10 million years virtually all the different phyla, or body types, came into being. (run-on) 5. The Burgess Shale in the Canadian Rockies contains countless fossils dating from the Cambrian period. *Some* animals found there have no living descendants. (run-on) 6. Others are primitive ancestors of animals still in existence. *A* lot of the animals look like something out of a horror movie! (run-on) 7. Among the strange fossil creatures *are* the tulip-shaped Dinomischus and Hallucigenia, a wormlike animal with spikes along its back and short spiky legs. (fragment) 8. Perhaps the most significant discovery among the fossils of the Burgess Shale is Pikaia. (sentence) 9. Pikaia *is* a worm no bigger than your pinky finger, with the beginnings of a spinal column. (fragment) 10. This unassuming little fellow is our own ancestor. *We* certainly have come a long way! (run-on)

SECTION THREE

Exercise 1 1. pitchers' 2. Navroz's 3. radios' 4. actress's 5. grandchildren's

Exercise 2 1. family's (*possessive singular*) 2. Haley's (*possessive singular*), people's (*possessive singular*) 3. generations (*plural*), changes (*plural*) 4. ancestors' (*possessive plural*) 5. results (*plural*) 6. historians' (*possessive plural*), world's (*possessive singular*) 7. ancestors (*plural*) 8. chances (*plural*)

SECTION FOUR

Exercise 1 1. We 2. she 3. they 4. me 5. he 6. him 7. I 8. us 9. her 10. she

Exercise 2 1. who 2. whom 3. who, whom 4. who 5. who 6. who 7. whom 8. who 9. whom 10. who

Exercise 3 1. himself 2. he 3. I 4. itself 5. itself 6. himself 7. it 8. itself 9. itself 10. himself

Exercise 4 1. their 2. travels, his or her 3. their 4. their 5. his or her 6. his or her 7. his 8. choose, their 9. have, themselves 10. their

Exercise 5 1. Your, you're 2. who's, his or her *Revised: "Tongue showing" is one of those signals; if you are sticking out the tip of your tongue you are sending the signal, "Don't bother me, I'm busy."* 3. who's *Revised: Children who are concentrating very hard on some task are likely to have their tongues sticking out.* 4. it's 5. who's, those *Revised: Even more curiously, people who receive those tongue showing signals will likely think twice before disturbing you, but they won't know what made them so cautious!*

Exercise 6 1. We 2. I 3. me 4. he 5. himself 6. whose 7. who 8. she 9. whom

SECTION FIVE

Exercise 1 1. extraordinary/evidence (*adjective*) 2. tirelessly/worked (*adverb*) 3. fabulous/temples; palaces, monuments, and fountains (*adjective*) 4. miserable/conditions (*adjective*) 5. cleverly/provided (*adverb*) 6. largely/built (*adverb*) 7. deeply/suffered (*adverb*) 8. uncontrollably/raged (*adverb*) 9. frequently/destroyed (*adverb*) 10. magnificently/survived (*adverb*)

Exercise 2 1. quickly 2. careful 3. suddenly 4. magnificent 5. dramatically 6. quickly 7. weak 8. fearful 9. wonderfully 10. perfect

Exercise 3 to try to paddle (*infinitive phrase/noun*), throwing our world into impenetrable darkness (*participial phrase/adjective*), in the canoe (*prepositional phrase/adjective*), awakening to Dana's sharp rebukes (*participial phrase/adjective*), thoroughly disoriented, and thoroughly lost (*participial phrase, adjective*), At about five (*prepositional phrase/ adverb*), to hallucinate (*infinitive phrase/noun*), After six hours of torment (*prepositional phrase/adverb*)

Exercise 4 1. favourite 2. more fun 3. better 4. more elegantly 5. grander 6. happier 7. biggest 8. greatest 9. interesting 10. unique

Exercise 5 1. well 2. well 3. bad 4. good 5. this 6. these 7. those 8. well 9. those 10. this

Exercise 6 1. When she was young, the Barry girl *was* interested in *nothing* but medicine.
2. Unfortunately, in the early 1800s it was *not possible* for women to study at university. **3.** She *could see no* other way to attain her goal, so she changed her name from Miranda to James, and disguised herself as a man. **4.** It *could hardly* have been easy, but she kept the disguise up for her whole life. **5.** People who met her *never guessed* her identity. **6.** She *was scarcely* ever seen without her white lapdog, Psyche. **7.** James Barry *never hesitated* to speak out against the conditions in leper colonies, prisons, and asylums she visited. (or *never did hesitate*) **8.** These institutions *were barely* fit for human habitation. **9.** In 1857, when James Barry was named inspector-general of Canada's military hospitals, there *was no* higher medical post in the country.

Exercise 7 1. *If you want* to see the Rockies up close, good boots and a compass will take you further than a car. **2.** The mountains come alive *when you are hiking along the trails.* **3.** I once saw a bear *as I was* walking along the trail in my hiking boots! **4.** To capture such moments, *I keep* my camera close at hand. **5.** This time, though, *I was still crouched in the bushes,* struggling with my lens cap, as the huge beast lumbered off into the forest.

Exercise 8 1. any **2.** beautiful **3.** larger **4.** higher **5.** really **6.** deepest **7.** most ancient **8.** well **9.** most difficult **10.** magnificent

SECTION SIX

Exercise 1 1. was (*linking*) **2.** called (*action; transitive*) **3.** is (*linking*) **4.** worshipped (*action; transitive*) **5.** protected (*action; transitive*) **6.** adored (*action; transitive*) **7.** took (*action; transitive*) **8.** grieved (*action; intransitive*) **9.** returned (*action; intransitive*) **10.** went (*action; intransitive*), was (*linking*), descended (*action; intransitive*), *was* (linking)

Exercise 2 1. freeze, freezing, froze, frozen **2.** tear, tearing, tore, torn

Exercise 3 1. had hoped **2.** was **3.** has delayed **4.** will, do **5.** has done **6.** will call **7.** works **8.** will have rewritten **9.** has, completed **10.** are

Exercise 4 1. Anyone with a home computer and a modem *can access computer networks.* **2.** *Subscribers can use* these networks to get information about everything from stock market reports to video selections. **3.** *People with similar interests can join* discussion groups, called newsgroups. **4.** correct **5.** The interesting thing about newsgroups is that *other users in the group can't see* your age, sex, and race.

6. correct **7.** Computer networks have serious uses as well; *coup leaders shut down* television and radio during the 1991 attempt to overthrow Mikhail Gorbachev. **8.** *Boris Yeltsin used* the Internet to get information and to maintain contact with the West. **9.** Some people worry that *networks will reduce* face-to-face human interaction. **10.** Also, *governments might abuse* the huge amount of information available through these "information superhighways."

Exercise 5 1. rising **2.** raising **3.** lying **4.** lies **5.** raised **6.** sat **7.** raised **8.** set **9.** laid

Exercise 6 1. In January of 1994, <u>an earthquake shook Los Angeles</u>, <u>killing many residents and causing extensive damage</u> to buildings and highways. **2.** Despite the devastation <u>that the early-morning quake brought,</u> you could say it *had chosen* a good time to happen. **3.** The day of the quake was a holiday, so traffic was light; the death toll would have *risen* dramatically if the tremors *had happened* on a regular working day. **4.** Los Angeles *sits* on the San Andreas fault, where two of the earth's plates meet. **5.** The epicentre of the quake *lay* in the San Fernando Valley, near Northridge. **6.** Anyone who figures out a way to pinpoint where and when the next earthquake will hit *will have made* an important discovery. **7.** Some Chinese studies *have shown* that animals *will run* from their lairs in the hours before a quake hits. **8.** Snakes that live underground will *rise* to the surface, even if the weather is cold enough to kill them. **9.** In Los Angeles, <u>many residents lost dogs</u> and <u>cats</u> just days before the quake *hit*. **10.** <u>Some scientists believe</u> that animals *know* when a quake *will occur* because they sense the changes in the earth's magnetic field.

SECTION SEVEN

Exercise 1 1. scare **2.** fear **3.** include **4.** need **5.** help **6.** explain **7.** learn **8.** helps **9.** give **10.** are

Exercise 2 1. wears, make **2.** think **3.** is **4.** look **5.** have **6.** is **7.** think **8.** are

Exercise 3 1. artists, were **2.** paintings, hang **3.** Everyone, recognizes **4.** Most, reflect **5.** Few, know **6.** Most, know **7.** many, were **8.** one, is **9.** technique, makes **10.** Everyone, understands

Exercise 4 1. love **2.** understands **3.** decide **4.** is **5.** is **6.** develop **7.** appear **8.** seem **9.** help **10.** know

Exercise 5 1. shoots **2.** is **3.** Was, was **4.** are **5.** Are **6.** are, are **7.** are **8.** appear, look, aren't **9.** Are **10.** is

Exercise 6 1. don't **2.** don't **3.** don't **4.** don't **5.** doesn't **6.** doesn't **7.** doesn't **8.** don't **9.** don't **10.** don't

SECTION EIGHT

Exercise 1 Note: Answers may vary. 1. Woolly mammoths lived over ten thousand years ago in North America, Europe, and Asia. (*simple sentence*) **2.** Long tusks *and enormous size* were characteristic of the mammoths. (*simple sentence*) **3.** Modern elephants stand about three metres high at the shoulder, *but* mammoths stood about four metres high. (*compound sentence*) **4.** Years ago, scientists in Siberia discovered *and excavated* a peculiar mammoth. (*simple sentence*) **5.** The mammoth was frozen, *and it had* buttercups in its mouth. (*compound sentence*) **6.** Thousands of years ago, something had frozen the mammoth *as well as* the plants. (*simple sentence*) **7.** The fresh green plants mean that the weather must have been warm, *but* the freezing mammoth required a sudden, fierce cold. (*compound sentence*) **8.** For years now, scientists *and crackpots* have speculated about what might have caused the sudden deep freeze of the Siberian mammoth. (*simple sentence*) **9.** To this day, no one has solved this mystery, *and no one even* has a clue as to how to go about solving it. (*compound sentence*) **10.** Somehow that mammoth *and those buttercups were* warm one moment and frozen solid the next moment! (*simple sentence*)

Exercise 2 1. This is a picture of a dog who meant a lot to me. **2.** The name that we gave him was Norman. **3.** Norman believed he was human. **4.** Although he was just a small brown mongrel, he thought he was very fierce. **5.** When we walked through the field with the cows in it, Norman would stand still and bark loudly. **6.** However, if a cow started to move toward him, he would start whimpering and run between our legs! **7.** Another time, at the lake, he barked indignantly at a piece of grass floating in the water whenever anyone was close enough to hear. **8.** When someone finally fished it out and laid it on the shore, he grabbed it and shook it until it was well and truly dead! **9.** On summer nights, his favourite place to sleep was in the barn, where it was cool. **10.** In winter, he spent his evenings on my bed, because he liked to make a nest out of my quilt.

SECTION NINE

Exercise 1 1. Europeans, Tibet, I, Parisian, Doctor Louis St Cyr **2.** China, Kunlun Mountains, Himalayas **3.** Chinese, Tibetan, Buddha, Buddhism, Dalai Lama, India **4.** non-Tibetans, Tibetan, Chinese **5.** I'll, Uncle Louis, Aunt Justine

Exercise 2 1. CN Tower, Toronto **2.** North America, Newfoundland **3.** West, West Edmonton Mall, Alberta **4.** North, Hudson Bay **5.** Pacific Ocean **6.** Mount Everest, Himalayas **7.** Sahara, North Africa **8.** Australia **9.** China **10.** Nile, Amazon

Exercise 3 1. Battle of the Plains of Abraham, September **2.** Oneida, Mohawk, Onondaga, Cayuga, Seneca, Tuscarora, Six Nations Confederacy **3.** Islam, Moslems, Muslims **4.** Canadians **5.** North Atlantic Treaty Organization

Exercise 4 1. Ancient History I, Business Math II, English **2.** A.M. (or a.m.), English, Shakespearean **3.** B.C. **4.** Ides **5.** Mars, Roman

Exercise 5
R.R.#3,
Scofield, B.C.
V6C 6C3
(604) 763 2425
Dear Severn Cullis-Suzuki:
I am a grade 9 student at *Scofield Secondary School*, and I am writing to tell you how much I enjoyed reading the speech you gave at the Earth Summit in *Rio Centro, Brazil.* You and your friends in the *Environmental Children's Organization* have inspired my friends and me to do something in our own high school to help the environment. I think you spoke for all young people when you said, *"You* are deciding what kind of world we will grow up in." I hope the delegates listened to you.
I am looking forward to reading your new book, *Tell the World.* I'm sure it will be full of good ideas. I saw it reviewed in our local paper, the *Sentinel,* but it hasn't shown up in the bookstores yet. My brother said that he would buy it for me for my birthday, which is on *May* 28.
I am enclosing a copy of *Earthwatch,* which is a magazine my friends and I produce and circulate around our school. We would like very much to interview you for our next edition. Is there any chance you would be free to talk to me on the phone for fifteen minutes or so in early *June*? Please let me know as soon as possible.
Sincerely yours,
Stella Sarmazian

SECTION TEN

Exercise 1 1. Look! Up in the sky! It's a bird, it's a plane, its...Superman! **2.** Have you been in a comic book store lately? **3.** If you haven't, look out. **4.** I was in one recently, and I asked the sales clerk if they carried any old Superman comics. **5.** She looked up sullenly from her portable CD player and pointed to the back of the store. **6.** I stood there browsing for a long time, until the clerk called out, "Are you planning on buying anything?" **7.** Hey! No one treats me, **B. J.** Klevering, like that! **8.** I looked her straight in the eye, straightened my rumpled collar, and asked, "Would you mind ringing in these two comics while I choose another?" **9.** At the cash, she said, "That will be **$53.23.** Would you like a bag?" **10.** Yikes! Unfortunately, I was too proud to back down, so if anyone wants to buy a vintage Superman Doomsday comic, please write to me at 7 Mill **St., apt.** 401, **Mtl.,** PQ H2W1C4.

Exercise 2 1. Theatresports, as its name suggests, is part theatre and part sports. **2.** It is another name for improvisational comedy, or improv for short. **3.** While the idea originated in Calgary in 1977, there are now groups in Calgary, Toronto, Halifax, and Vancouver, as well as in countries around the world. **4.** Here is how it works: First, players divide into two teams; second, they ask the audience for a word, phrase, or sentence to start the game off; third, each team steps out on stage and starts to improvise. **5.** Although a panel of judges decides which team is the winner, the audience can make its feelings known by laughing, yelling, and throwing foam-rubber boo-bricks. **6.** Anything can happen at a Theatresports performance: when we went, a man in the audience lost his head, jumped up on stage, and started yodelling! **7.** However, the players didn't miss a beat: they simply incorporated the yodeller into their skit. **8.** Yes, some skits bomb completely and some go on too long, but some are just hilarious. **9.** A lot of successful, well established comedians, including Martin Short and The Kids in the Hall, began their careers with Theatresports. **10.** Remember, Theatresports often runs workshops on improv for the public, so you, too, can discover your hidden talent as a comedian!

Exercise 3 1. If you must insult someone, do it with style. **2.** There is a fine art to battling someone with words, and you would do well to learn from the masters. **3.** In ancient Greece, the statesman Demosthenes once told one of his enemies, Phocion, that the citizens of Athens would kill him one day when they were in a rage. **4.** "And you when they are in their senses," replied Phocion. **5.** "You little pipsqueak," an angry voter once yelled at former Saskatchewan Premier Tommy Douglas, "I could swallow you in one bite." **6.** "And if you did, my friend, you'd have more brains in your belly than you have in your head," quipped Douglas. **7.** Groucho Marx, the famous comedian, once said, "I've had a wonderful evening, but this wasn't it." **8.** correct **9.** Dorothy Parker, a critic and author, wrote

in a book review, "This is not a novel to be tossed aside lightly; it should be thrown with great force." **10.** Finally, someone once described journalist Clifford Makins as "A legend in his own lunchtime."

Exercise 4
Friday, October 14, 1994
Dear Myra,
Would you please send me the Shums's new address? Somehow I've managed to lose the piece of paper Allan gave me that contained all the information about their move. I can't imagine what I did with it, but wherever it's gone, gone it is. I'd appreciate any help you can give me.
Your friend,
Theo
Wednesday, October 19, 1994
Dear Theo,
    I'm happy to give you what information I have about the Shums's address. Unfortunately, it isn't very accurate. Lydia left me a note with her new address before she left, but she was in a hurry, and her handwriting is hard to read. I know it says Church Street; the question is, is that a 1 or a 7 in their street number? Seven, I'd say, but don't hold me to it. The note says:
As of October 10, 1994, our new address is (1 or 7?) Church St., Nanaimo, BC V6C 1E5.
    Let me know if you have any luck. I know Allan will be anxious to hear from you.
Your friend,
Myra

Exercise 5
Mr. Raffi Armenian
R.R.1
Sioux Lookout, Ont.
M6Y 2Y5
Monday, June 6, 1994
Dear Raffi,
    I just thought I'd drop you a line to let you know we got home safely, and that we really enjoyed seeing you for the weekend. Thanks for your hospitality.
    Raffi, remember when you said those country roads could be scary at night? How right you were! We had quite an adventure on the way home. At about 10:00 p.m., we were all telling scary stories when the car got a flat tire! It was dark, of course, and we didn't have a flashlight. Nevertheless, Reza, Nish, and I all clambered out and started fumbling around; since the car belonged to Reza's dad, we weren't sure where the jack was. No one paid much attention to Mickey, our Old English Sheepdog.
    The moon was full, but the trees on both

sides of the road were so dense it seemed almost pitch black. Suddenly, there was a movement of branches, and a strange figure appeared from the trees. With the moon behind it, it looked like something from the planet Mars, with spikes all over and two antennae on its head!

So what did we do? First, we gasped; second, we screamed; and third, we ran like blazes! Nish stopped running first, because her shoe fell off. She looked back, sniffed, and then started laughing. "Here, boy," she called, and the creature started slinking toward us.

Of course, it was Mickey, who had wandered off into the woods and rolled in something old, dead, and very smelly. Some branches had stuck in his hair, and that was what had looked, at least to our impressionable minds, like antennae. He was so ashamed of himself he stayed perfectly quiet and didn't even try to chase us.

Once the tire was on, we got out of there as fast as we could, and we sang rousing songs the rest of the way home to keep our minds off the dark and aliens. Unfortunately, we had to drive with the windows open and Mickey lying morosely in the hatchback. We aired the car out overnight and sprayed it with air freshener, but Reza's dad still asked what we had done to leave such an awful smell.

Talk to you soon, I hope. If you feel like dropping me a line, my address is 1041 Macmillan Ave., Winnipeg, MB O1O 3G2.

Your friend,

Sami

P.S. Mickey, by the way, is now clean as a whistle, and he promises never to wander into the woods again.

Exercise 6

Dear Sir:

I am writing to apply for the position of Senior Counsellor at Camp Wombat, which was advertised on the bulletin board at my school. My qualifications for this position include the follow-/ing: three summers' experience, first as a camper and then as a junior counsellor, at Camp Chachabonga; a love of sports; and well-developed leadership skills.

My three years at Camp Chachabonga taught me a lot about leadership and responsibility: as a junior counsellor I was res-/ponsible for ten campers ranging in age from 7 to 9 years old. The camp catered to both able-bodied campers and those with physical disabilities: one-third of all the campers were in wheel-chairs, including three of my charges. I learned another important skill at Chachabonga: self-discipline. When you are in charge of rousing ten sleepy campers from their beds at 5:00 a.m. to go

hiking, you need lots of self-discipline!

I would greatly enjoy working as a Senior Counsellor at Camp Wombat this summer; moreover, I believe I have a lot to offer both the campers and the other staff members: enthusiasm, effort, and a sense of fun!

I have attached a copy of my résumé. Please feel free to call me to arrange an interview. I look forward to meeting you.

Exercise 7 1. There are two *s's* in the word "dessert" when it refers to sweets eaten after a meal. **2.** *That's* easy for me to remember, because there are two words in my favourite *dessert's* name: ice cream. **3.** Did you know that Häagen *Dazs's* name is made up? **4.** *It's* not from Scandinavia; its birthplace is the Bronx! **5.** Häagen *Dazs's creator's* name is Bill Mattus, but *he's* since sold the company to Pillsbury. **6.** *Here's* another piece of ice cream trivia: ice cream sundaes got their name because, back in the *'90s* of the last century, it was considered wrong to sip sodas on Sundays. **7.** The soda fountain *owners'* response was to concoct an ice cream dish without the soda, and sundaes were born. **8.** *Canadians'* feelings toward ice cream are made clear by the fact that we are the fourth largest consumers of ice cream in the world. **9.** Ice cream may not be *everyone's* favourite, but I *don't* know anyone who *can't* stand it. **10.** *It's* certainly popular at *children's* parties!

Exercise 8 1. <u>Bugle</u>, "Famous Last Words," **2.** <u>Cinderella</u>, <u>Rapunzel</u> **3.** "And they lived happily ever after." **4.** <u>Casablanca</u> **5.** "Louis," says Rick, "I think this is the beginning of a beautiful friendship." **6.** <u>Invasion of the Body Snatchers</u> **7.** <u>The Prisoner</u> **8.** "Fallout," **9.** <u>Gone with the Wind</u> **10.** "After all, tomorrow is another day"?

Index